Hilarious
Roasts,
Toasts &
One-Liners

Hilarious
Roasts,
Toasts &
One·Liners

GENE PERRET
with Terry Martin

GALAHAD BOOKS
NEW YORK

Previously published in two separate volumes as:

ROASTS & TOASTS
Copyright ©1997 by Gene Perret and Terry Perret Martin

THE LITTLE GIANT ENCYCLOPEDIA OF ONE LINERS
Copyright © 1999 by Gene Perret and Terry Perret Martin.

All rights reserved. No part of this work may be reproduced or transmitted in any form or by any means, electronic or mechanical, including photocopying, recording, or any information storage and retrieval system, without permission in writing from: Sterling Publishing Company, Inc., 387 Park Avenue South, New York, NY 10016.

First Galahad Books edition pubished in 2001.

Galahad Books
A division of BBS Publishing Corporation
450 Raritan Center Parkway
Edison, New Jersey 08837

Galahad Books is a registered trademark of BBS Publishing Corporation.

Published by arrangement with Sterling Publishing Company, Inc.

Distributed by Sterling Publishing Company, Inc.
387 Park Avenue South
New York, NY 10016
Distributed in Canada by Sterling Publishing
Canadian Manda Group
One Atlantic Avenue, Suite 105
Toronto, Ontario, Canada M6K 3E7

Library of Congress Catalog Card number: 00-136108

ISBN: 1-57866-123-4

Printed in the United States of America.

CONTENTS

Hilarious
Roasts
&Toasts

For my Sophia
　　　　—Grandpop

For Little Miss Sophia
　　　　—Mommy

For consistency and simplicity, the authors used male pronouns where there was a choice throughout this book. Readers, though, can easily adapt most of the jokes to apply to either men or women.

CONTENTS

**YOU ARE CORDIALLY
INVITED TO**

LET THE ROAST BEGIN

We gather here in friendship. A toast to good friends: Each time you become one, you gain one.

A toast to friendship: Not all of us can love our enemies, but we can all treat our friends a little better.

When our journey through this lifetime ends, the richest are those with many friends.

Here's to our toastmaster for the evening: A toastmaster is a person who eats a meal he doesn't want so he can get up and tell a lot of stories he doesn't remember to people who've already heard them.
—*George Jessel*

IRREVERENT INTRODUCTIONS

Why don't the feller who says, "I'm not a speechmaker," let it go at that instead of giving a demonstration?   —*Kin Hubbard*

A speech is like a love affair. Any fool can start it, but to end it requires considerable skill.   —*Lord Mancroft*

He hasn't got much to say, but at least he doesn't try to say anything else.   —*Robert Benchley*

Here's a speaker who needs no introduction. Believe me, we've tried several and they don't help.

• • •

You've heard of many speakers who need no introduction. Here's a speaker who doesn't deserve one.

• • •

Let's bring our next speaker on with a great big hand. It may be the only one he gets all night.

. . .

I could say many nice things about our next speaker, but I'd rather be honest.

. . .

You're in for a special treat tonight. Our next speaker has promised to keep it short.

. . .

This next gentleman is not a professional speaker and you'll have the opportunity this evening to see why.

. . .

There are some speakers who need no introduction. But our next speaker needs all the help he can get.

. . .

Our next speaker is one who keeps listeners on the edge of their seat. What happens is many of them doze off and slide forward.

. . .

Our next speaker is a man who has received so many accolades that he finally had to look the word up in the dictionary.

. . .

I've heard it said about our next speaker that no matter what you pay him, he's worth every penny of it. He's speaking here tonight for free.

. . . So don't get your hopes up.

. . .

Our next speaker needs no introduction—especially not the ridiculously inflated one that he wrote here.

. . .

What can I say about our next speaker ... that wouldn't make us look foolish for bringing him here?

. . .

What can I say about our next speaker that he probably hasn't already said about himself?

. . .

And now our final speaker of the evening. You've often heard the expression "last but not least." Tonight is the exception to that rule.

. . .

Our next speaker not only needs no introduction, it probably wouldn't do any good.

. . .

We searched high and low for an interesting speaker for this evening. We found our next speaker during the low part of the search.

. . .

This gentleman is one of the most sought-after speakers in the country. But enough about his outstanding bench warrants.

. . .

Many of you have heard our next speaker before. We appreciate your sacrifice in being here anyway.

. . .

People on our committee said, "We want an entertaining speaker. Get (*name of speaker*)." I said to them, "Make up your minds."

. . .

It's not easy finding entertaining and enlightening speakers for these events. So now I'd like to present to you, straight from the bottom of the barrel ...

. . .

I talked to members of other associations and they were delighted that we had booked this next speaker for our meeting. It meant that their group didn't have to book him.

. . .

As you all know, we don't pay our speakers much. I'm happy to say this next gentleman is worth every penny of it.

. . .

I always look for one outstanding trait to feature when introducing a speaker. So, please welcome a speaker now who fits into our price range.

AFTER A BAD INTRODUCTION

I could stand up here and be very funny, but I don't want to change the format of your show.
—*Jack E. Leonard*

I've always wanted to be one of those speakers who needs no introduction—especially after receiving one like that.

. . .

When I was a kid I had a puppy dog who ran away. That had always been the worst day of my life . . . until tonight's introduction.

. . .

I don't know whether I've just been introduced or read my Miranda rights.

. . .

I've never received an introduction like that before. And if my lawyer is worth his salt, I'll never receive one like that again.

. . .

Thank you, I'm happy to be here . . . having survived that introduction.

. . .

Thank you. I'm happy to be here. After that introduction, I'm happy to be anywhere.

. . .

Thank you. I must tell you, I've received much worse introductions than that . . . and from much better people.

. . .

Unfortunately for me, that was a terrible introduction. Unfortunately for you, it was appropriate for my presentation.

. . .

When people ask me, "Who would you like to introduce you?" I generally say, "Oh anybody." After this evening I'm going to say, "Oh, anybody except . . ."

. . .

I'm always worried that the introduction is going to make promises to the audience that I, as a speaker, cannot live up to. No problem with that tonight.

. . .

[*Name of introducer*] talked to me earlier and said, "What would you like me to say in your introduction?" I said, "Use your own good judgment." That's the last time I'll make that mistake.

. . .

I thought that was a very creative and funny introduction. I can't wait to call my attorney to see if he agrees with me.

What a wonderful introduction. I just hope it doesn't put me into a higher tax bracket.
—*Bob Hope*

That was a wonderful introduction. Now even I can't wait to hear what I say.

. . .

That's a fantastic introduction. If I had known I was that good, I would have charged more.

. . .

That's probably the best introduction I've ever received in my whole life—except for one time when the host said, "Why don't you just stand up and introduce yourself."

. . .

I wish my parents could have heard that glorious introduction. My Dad would have been so proud. And my Mom, God bless her, would have probably believed most of it.

. . .

That was a terrific introduction. In fact, in the middle of it, I turned to the person next to me and said, "Who is he talking about?"

". . . I'd like to meet the guy."

. . .

That was a very eloquent introduction. The problem is: it was so well done, now it's going to make my speech look bad.

. . .

I've always believed the best introduction was just to tell the simple truth about a person. But I liked this much better.

. . .

That introduction was very flattering. When I go to meet my Maker, could you come along with me?

. . .

That's the most flattering introduction I've ever received. And you read it just the way I wrote it.

. . .

That was a very gracious introduction. In fact, I'm sorry I have to speak now. I'd rather sit here all night and listen to your introduction.

. . .

Boy, if I had known I was going to get such a magnificent introduction, I would have brought along a better speech.

THE GUEST OF HONOR'S FAMILY

You know, you have very beautiful children. It's a good thing your wife cheats.
—*Joey Bishop*

We don't want our guest of honor's family to be shocked by some of the things we say tonight. We're only kidding. Besides, a lot of the nice things we say about him aren't true, either.

• • •

Our guest of honor has his entire family here with him tonight. You know how hard it is to get a baby-sitter once the children get into their twenties.

• • •

Right here, at the beginning of the program, I'd like to introduce the members of our guest of honor's family. By the time we get done with him, they may no longer want to be associated with him.

• • •

As you can see, our guest of honor is very fortunate to have such charming children, none of whom look like him.

• • •

Our guest of honor has his entire family with him tonight. But that's not going to stop us. We've still got them outnumbered.

• • •

We invited our guest of honor's family to be here with him tonight. We had to have someone sit at his table.

• • •

14

I'd like to warn our guest of honor's family that we are going to do a lot of bad jokes about him. We don't do it because we want to. It's just that with him, it's so easy.

· · ·

I spoke with one of our guest of honor's sons before the dinner. He told me he always wanted to grow up to be just like his Dad. I think tonight may change his mind.

· · ·

Our guest of honor wanted to have his family with him tonight—as character witnesses.

· · ·

Our guest of honor's family is here tonight, but they know him as a husband and a father. They don't know him as a working man. Come to think of it, neither do we.

· · ·

Our guest of honor is a husband, a father, and to us, a coworker. I'm sure he's a wonderful husband and father. And two out of three is not bad.

· · ·

I spoke to a member of our guest of honor's family before the banquet. He said, "I know this is a roast, but go easy on my Dad." I want the entire family to understand that no matter how cruel the jokes may sound, no matter how vicious the insults may seem, in your father's case, we are still going easy.

THE GUEST OF HONOR

They never give you a dinner—until you don't need one.
—*Will Rogers*

I think the world of you . . . and you know what I think of the world.
—*Henny Youngman*

We've had fun with our guest of honor tonight. And he sat there patiently while his wife explained the jokes to him.

. . .

Tradition dictates that we give our guest of honor the last word. However, tradition has no idea how dull he is.

. . .

Our speakers this evening have tried to be clever, funny, and entertaining. Now it's our guest of honor's turn. Unfortunately he's none of those things.

. . .

We've had a lot of fun here tonight. Now for a change of pace, I introduce our guest of honor.

. . .

We've taken great liberties with our guest of honor tonight. We've kidded him, taunted him, insulted him, but we feel we can do it with a guy like him because he has very little idea of what's going on.

. . .

We're now going to give our guest of honor equal time. But because he's such a dull guy, it will seem much longer.

. . .

I'll give you an idea of what kind of guy our guest of honor is. I leaned over to him a minute ago and said, "We're now going to give you a chance to respond to all of this." He said to me, "You mean they've been talking about me all night?"

. . .

Right now I'd like to introduce a prince of a guy, a hard worker, a great personality. I'd like to introduce that person, but instead I have to introduce our guest of honor.

. . .

I'd like to introduce a person now who has been a real good sport throughout this entire evening. Either that or he has absolutely no concept of what's going on.

. . .

We've had a lot of fun here tonight, but all good things must come to an end. With that in mind, I introduce our guest of honor.

. . .

We've said a lot of silly things this evening. We've poked fun, we've exaggerated. Now it's our guest of honor's turn to stand up and show you that we weren't that far off.

. . .

We've poked a lot of fun at our guest of honor tonight, but deep down inside we know that we didn't do half the stuff we could have. Now it's his turn.

. . .

I've been to a lot of these roasts and I've heard merciless jokes told about a lot of people, but I can truthfully say that never before have I seen a guest of honor who was so worthy of them.

. . . Here he is now to show you what I mean.

CELEBRATING

OUR GUEST OF HONOR

Dislikes People

Refuses Advice

Is Opinionated

Is a Procrastinator

Is an Optimist

Is a Pessimist

Is Absent-Minded

Needs Some Manners

Could Have Been a Diplomat

To our guest of honor! You've heard the expression "To know him is to love him." Our guest of honor has heard it, too.

Please raise your glasses and drink to our guest of honor. Why? Because it's as good an excuse as any.

We come here tonight to pay homage to our guest of honor. The word *homage* may be a little strong, but he doesn't care because so is what he's been drinking.

To our guest of honor! The nicest thing we can say about him is that he's a friend.

DISLIKES PEOPLE

Why be influenced by a person when you already are one?
—*Martin Mull*

Popularity is the easiest thing in the world to gain and the hardest to hold. —*Will Rogers*

I like to reminisce with people I don't know. Granted it takes a little longer. —*Steven Wright*

Nobody liked me because I was too popular. —*Jackie Vernon*

Our guest of honor feels this way about people: if it weren't for them, we wouldn't have to worry about traffic.

. . . or deodorant.

Our guest of honor just doesn't like people. When he goes to a party, he stays in the room with the coats.

. . .

19

He has an answering machine that says, "At the sound of the beep, hang up."

. . .

You must admit that people can sometimes be annoying; so, our guest of honor just tries to get in his shots first.

. . .

According to our guest of honor, the world's problems started when Adam and Eve decided to have children.

. . .

He has to learn that people aren't perfect, but they're the best company we've got.

. . .

He learned it from his uncle. His uncle enjoyed being alone so much, he formed the Hermit's Association.

. . . but he was the only one who showed up at the meetings.

. . .

He plans on going to heaven when he dies. He hates crowds.

. . .

It's an interesting philosophical question: If there were no people on earth, would humankind be better or worse off?

. . .

There would be no wars if there were no people. Who would we shoot at?

. . .

He once wanted to form a club for people like himself—the Perfect People's Association. But he sent out the invitations without stamps.

REFUSES ADVICE

I always pass on good advice. It is the only thing to do with it. It is never any use to oneself. —*Oscar Wilde*

It's better to keep your mouth shut and appear stupid than to open it and remove all doubt. —*Mark Twain*

It's always a silly thing to give advice, but to give good advice is absolutely fatal. —*Oscar Wilde*

When I get one of those "mom" headaches, I take the advice on the aspirin bottle. Take two and keep away from children. —*Roseanne Barr*

Advice is a drug in the market: the supply always exceeds the demands. —*Josh Billings*

Here's some advice my mother gave me ... trust your husband, adore your husband, and get as much as you can in your own name. —*Joan Rivers*

Never mind what I told you, do what I tell you. —*W. C. Fields*

Advice: the smallest current coin. —*Ambrose Bierce*

When a man comes to me for advice, I find out the kind of advice he wants, and I give it to him. —*Josh Billings*

Put all your eggs in one basket—and watch that basket. —*Mark Twain*

Our guest of honor feels about advice that it's truly better to give than to receive.

. . .

The only advice his mother ever gave him was "Don't have children."

. . .

He believes the best things in life are free—except for advice.

. . .

I agree with our guest of honor. I've been suspicious of advice ever since someone who was worse off than me told me how to better myself.

. . .

Our guest of honor believes the only advice to listen to is from wealthy, successful, powerful people. But then, what would they be doing talking to him?

. . .

He claims the best advice he ever got was "Don't listen to advice."
. . . he listened.

. . .

There's good advice and there's bad advice. If you're giving it, it's good; if you're listening to it, it's bad.

. . .

Most people ask for advice because they just want to hear someone else say what they're thinking.

. . .

Good advice is like the bottle of bitters you keep in the bar. It lasts a lifetime because you hardly ever use it.

. . .

Our guest of honor says a piece of advice should be like the common cold. If you've got a good one, keep it to yourself.

. . .

Be careful giving advice to people. It's the only commodity where if it's good, people get mad at you because it wasn't better.

IS OPINIONATED

When I need your opinion, I'll give it to you.   —*Sam Levenson*

Public opinion in this country runs like a shower. We have no temperatures between hot and cold.   —*Heywood Broun*

Loyalty to petrified opinions never yet broke a chain or freed a human soul.   —*Mark Twain*

It is not best that we shall all think alike; it is difference of opinion that makes horse races.   —*Mark Twain*

Yes, our guest of honor is opinionated, but if people didn't have different opinions, Baskin-Robbins could have gotten by with just one flavor.

. . .

Our guest of honor has an opinion; you and I have a stupid argument.

. . .

It's important to remember: one doesn't have to think to form an opinion.

. . .

Just because there are two sides to every argument doesn't mean either one is right.

. . .

If people held on to their principles the way they hold on to their opinion, this world would be a better place.

. . .

Opinions are like children. We always think ours are the best.

. . .

Differing opinions can make for an interesting debate, except in hockey, where it usually makes for a five-minute major penalty.

. . .

I've told our guest of honor often: "I respect your opinion. It's you I don't like."

. . .

Our guest of honor is entitled to his own opinion. What bothers him is when people think they're entitled to theirs, too.

. . .

Our guest of honor has already formed his opinion. Please don't distract him now with facts.

. . .

Anyone can have an opinion. Only those who agree with him can have a correct opinion.

. . .

Argument-ender: I will defend to the death your right to have an opinion, but I must warn you—you're getting dangerously close to that point.

IS A PROCRASTINATOR

Do not put off till tomorrow what can be put off till the day after tomorrow just as well.   —*Mark Twain*

Don't put off until tomorrow what you can do today. There may be a tax on it by then.   —*Milton Berle*

My mother said, "You won't amount to anything because you procrastinate." I said, "Just wait."   —*Judy Tenuta*

He who hesitates is a fool.   —*Mae West*

Our guest of honor claims he's not a procrastinator, but he hopes to be someday.

. . .

Our guest of honor told his wife, "Don't plan anything for this Fourth of July. I don't want to miss the Procrastinator's Christmas Party again this year."

. . .

In his biography our guest of honor wrote, "I'm definitely a precrastinator . . . a procastineater . . . a precrestinater. . . . Someday I'm going to learn how to spell that word."

. . .

Do you know what a nudist is? A person who wears hand-me-downs from a procrastinator.

. . .

Our guest of honor enjoys procrastination. It gives him something to do tomorrow.

. . .

Our guest of honor got good news today from the Procrastinators Society of America. The results of the election are in. He was president last year.

. . .

Our guest of honor is a procrastinator. He was going to quit the Procrastinators Society, but he never got around to it.

. . .

To a procrastinator, *today* is Latin for "my day off."

. . .

The invitations to the Annual Procrastinators Ball, which was held two months ago, were mailed out today.

. . . At the bottom they read, "Please send regrets only if you weren't here."

. . .

I may be a procrastinator or I may not be. I've just never gotten around to looking up that word in the dictionary.

. . .

Our guest of honor has a beautiful sign that reads, "Do it now." But he hasn't hung it up over his desk yet.

IS AN OPTIMIST

Optimist: Day-dreamer more elegantly spelled.   —*Mark Twain*

Definition of an *optimist:* A 94-year-old man who marries a 24-year-old girl and starts looking for a nice home close to a school.
                    —*Woody Woodbury*

An optimist is a guy who looks forward to the great scenery on a detour.   —*Milton Berle*

Our guest of honor is an optimist. An optimist is the kind of a person who will believe campaign speeches.

. . . even ones he makes himself.

. . .

An optimist is a person who buys something with a 90-day-warranty and expects it to work perfectly on the 91st day.

. . .

Optimism sees the bright side of everything—even pessimism.

. . .

I don't know what I am. I'd like to be an optimist, but I have a bad feeling about it.

. . .

It's easy to spot an optimist. He's the one wearing sunglasses in a thunderstorm.

. . .

A really great salesman is one who can sell an umbrella to an optimist.

. . .

You show an optimist the dark side of the moon and he'll see the bright side of it.

. . .

An optimist can see the good in everybody. The rest of us just don't have the time to look that hard.

. . .

Optimists are the cheerleaders of life.

. . .

The worst part about arguing with an optimist is, even if you win, he's happy.

. . .

Optimists like happy endings. That's why you'll rarely see a Southern optimist reading a Civil War novel.

Life is divided into the horrible and the miserable.

—*Woody Allen*

Things are going to get a lot worse before they get worse.

—*Lily Tomlin*

I told my psychiatrist that everyone hates me. He said I was being ridiculous—everyone hasn't met me yet.　　—*Rodney Dangerfield*

Our guest of honor is definitely a pessimist. A pessimist is a guy who would say, "Monday I hit the lottery for $2 million. Tuesday I won $100,000 at the track. Today, nothing."

. . .

A pessimist is a guy who hates all good things because he knows they must come to an end.

. . .

The pessimist and the optimist refused to marry because they couldn't decide how to raise the children.

The optimist was sure they'd turn out to be happy children; the pessimist wasn't sure they'd turn out to be children.

. . .

A pessimist is a person who carries a rabbit's foot to remind him how much luck it brought to the rabbit.

. . .

When things really can't get any worse, a pessimist finds some way to think they can.

. . .

An optimist sees the glass as half-full. The pessimist complains about what it's half-full *of*.

. . .

A pessimist will sit there and curse the darkness rather than light one little candle and then sit there and curse the light.

. . .

Our guest of honor is the kind of guy who, if he goes to a picnic where there are no ants, he thinks it's because the potato salad is no good.

. . .

Our guest of honor is someone who knows the movie is going to be lousy, but he goes anyway because he likes to complain about the popcorn.

. . .

You should always have a pessimist as your best man. That way the bride's parents might be glad she married you.

. . . unless they're both pessimists, too.

IS ABSENT-MINDED

There was an absent-minded professor who saw the sign he put on his door that said, "Back in thirty minutes." So he sat down to wait.
—*Milton Berle*

There are three signs of old age. One is loss of memory. The other two I forget.
—*Bob Hope*

Have you heard the one about the executive who was so old that when he chased his secretary around the desk, he couldn't remember why?
—*Larry Wilde*

Our guest of honor is so absent-minded, on Easter morning he can hide his own eggs.

. . .

Our guest of honor not only forgets names and faces, but the difference between the two.

. . .

Our guest of honor is so absent-minded, at the beginning of each workday he writes his name on a piece of paper. That's so at the middle of the workday, he'll remember who he is.

. . .

Our guest of honor is so absent-minded, he answers every question the same way: "What was the question?"

. . .

He's so forgetful that he's a real slow reader because everytime he turns the page, he forgets why.

. . .

Someone asked our guest of honor to pass the salt and pepper. He said, "Here's the pepper. Now what was that first thing you asked for?"

. . .

At work, we call him "Frothy" because after he brushes his teeth in the morning, he forgets to rinse.

. . .

He makes new friends easily. He has to . . . he can't remember the old ones.

. . .

The company takes advantage of his forgetfulness. He's worked here about thirty years. Management says in five or six more years they'll hold his 25th anniversary party.

. . .

He's very absent-minded. He never makes the same mistake twice . . . as far as he's concerned.

. . .

I asked our guest of honor once when his birthday was. He said, "Sometime this year."

. . .

Our guest of honor has two friends who are just as absent-minded as he is. Their favorite pastime is to get together and then one of them leaves. The other two try to guess which one left.

NEEDS SOME MANNERS

Good breeding consists in concealing how much we think of ourselves and how little we think of the other person.

—*Mark Twain*

It's gotten so that if a man opens a door for a lady to go through first, he's the doorman.
—*Mae West*

He's so polite, his tombstone will read, "Pardon me for not standing."
—*Milton Berle*

He was a gentleman all over; and so was his family. He was well born, as the saying is, and that's worth as much in a man as it is in a horse.
—*Mark Twain*

I'm always a gentleman. Whenever I see an empty seat on a bus, I point it out to a lady. Then I race her for it.
—*Henny Youngman*

Our guest of honor believes that etiquette is for highbrows. If you can't spell it, you don't need it.

. . .

At the kind of restaurants he goes to, the only rule of etiquette is not to tell anyone what's in the secret sauce.

. . .

Our guest of honor's mom said to him at an early age, "Don't you want to learn to be polite and refined?" He said, "No, thank you."

. . .

His brothers and sisters always had good manners at the dinner table—at least until the food fight broke out.

. . .

His mom kept repeating, "Don't put your elbows on the table. Don't put your elbows on the table." He grew up assuming all other parts of the body were OK.

. . .

His table manners are atrocious. I know chicken can be eaten with your fingers, but not when it's in soup.

. . .

My mother always said she wanted her children to act like little ladies and gentlemen, which was confusing for us since we were all boys.

. . .

My mother had a rule at the table: no one could start eating until everyone was served. Some people would call that etiquette; she called it a fair fight.

. . .

My mom would say, "If you don't have good manners how do you ever expect to have dinner at the White House?" I'd say, "I could be elected President."

. . .

My mom always said that good manners were just common sense. But so was getting to the meat loaf before my brother Jimmy got to it.

. . .

At our house, we had another word for good table manners—*starvation.*

. . .

It's always considered bad taste to spell out naughty words with your alphabet soup before eating it.

COULD HAVE BEEN A DIPLOMAT

That's called diplomacy, doing just what you said you wouldn't.
—*Will Rogers*

A diplomat is a man who can convince his wife she looks bad in a mink.
—*Milton Berle*

You can diplomat America out of almost everything she has, but don't try to bluff her.
—*Will Rogers*

To make a good salad is to be a brilliant diplomatist. The problem is entirely the same in both cases. To know exactly how much oil one must put with one's vinegar.
—*Oscar Wilde*

Our guest of honor likes to think of himself as a diplomat. Diplomacy can sometimes be the art of looking someone in the eye and stabbing them in the back at the same time.

. . .

Diplomacy is the art of being able to cut someone's legs out from under them and still leave them standing on their own two feet.

. . .

Diplomacy is the art of giving the other guy exactly what he wants, whether he wants it or not.

. . .

Diplomacy would be like Pinocchio telling a lie and not even having his nose know it.

. . .

A diplomat is a salesman with a sash across his chest.

. . .

A diplomat is someone who can tell you good news and bad news, and you can't tell the difference.

. . .

Saying, "No, you can't have that" is dictatorial. Getting the other guy to say, "No, I don't want that" is diplomacy.

. . .

Diplomacy is when you steal from someone, instead of saying, "Stop, thief!" they say, "Thank you."

. . .

Diplomacy is being born with a silver fork in your mouth instead of a forked tongue.

. . .

A diplomat is the only person who can say to an opponent, "Congratulations, you lose."

. . .

A diplomat is the only person who can report to his boss, "I've spoken with the enemy and I think I've got them exactly where they want us."

. . .

Diplomacy is the art of winning without having the other guy lose.

A SPECIAL ROAST FOR

FeLLoW WoRKeRS

The Boss

A Coworker

A Hard Worker

Not a Hard Worker

A Talker

A Party Guy

To my fellow workers:
  We've made some profit.
  We've made some loss.
  We've made them both,
  Despite our boss.

To my fellow workers:
  To those who toil hard in the workplace
  I raise my glass on high.
  To those who gave their all for the company,
  Here's a toast to me and one other guy.

To my fellow workers:
  We work in the trenches
  Day after day.
  Your friendship makes it worthwhile.
  It's certainly not the pay.

THE BOSS

A good executive never puts off until tomorrow what he can get you to do today.   *—Joey Adams*

A good executive is a man who believes in sharing the credit with the man who did the work.   *—Joey Adams*

A vice-president in an advertising agency is a "molehill man"—that's an executive who comes to work at 9 A.M. and finds a molehill on his desk—and by 5 P.M. he makes it into a mountain.   *—Fred Allen*

Everything he touches turns to gold. I'm afraid to go to the toilet with him.   *—Milton Berle*

The boss, what an idiot. I told him how to run the company. We parted good friends, though. He boarded his yacht and I took the subway home.   *—George Jessel*

This is a new experience for me—saying things about our boss in front of his face.

. . .

This is a night for all of us to gather together to honor our boss, share a meal and a few drinks with him, and in general, pretend that we like him.

. . .

They asked me to say a few words about our boss. My mom always taught me if you can't say something nice about a person, don't say anything at all. So, if you'll all join me now in a moment of silence . . .

. . .

It's easy to say nice things about our boss. About his leadership, his fairness, his understanding. That's easy. The hard part is keeping the straight face.

. . .

I wanted to say about our boss that he was born to lead, to pull his share of the load, to be a working part of the team. Then it dawned on me that you could say those same things about a Siberian husky.

. . . and they're friendlier.

. . .

Our boss was never too busy to be sympathetic when we were in trouble. He always gave us a cold shoulder to cry on.

. . .

I wouldn't say our boss was tough, but periodically he'd go to a palmist to get his brass knuckles read.

. . .

Our boss was always ready to listen to our troubles. But then, why shouldn't he? He caused most of them.

. . .

Our boss told us from day one that his door was always open. And it was. It wasn't until recently that we found out that was by order of the fire marshal.

. . .

I remember our boss philosophizing: "Happiness in life is something to do, someone to love, and something to hope for." Then he'd add, "Now get the hell to work."

. . .

Our boss often told me his secretaries couldn't keep their hands off him. It was true. They all wanted to choke him.

. . .

And our boss is clumsy. He wanted us all to put our best foot forward, but he kept tripping over it.

. . .

Whenever we had troubles that we wanted to discuss with the boss, he'd listen and have those three words that we all came to know: "Like I care."

A COWORKER

She's the kind of girl who climbed the ladder of success wrong by wrong.
—*Mae West*

Someday you'll go far and I hope you'll stay there.
—*Henny Youngman*

There's absolutely nothing our guest of honor wouldn't do for this company and there's absolutely nothing the company wouldn't do for him. That pretty much sums up their relationship. All these years they've done absolutely nothing for each other.

. . .

I've been our guest of honor's best friend for many, many years, and quite frankly, I think it's someone else's turn.

. . .

What do you say about someone whom you've sat next to in the office for so many years. Three words come to mind: "Do some work."

. . .

If you have trouble in the office, you can go to our guest of honor. If you have problems at home, you can talk to him. If you have troubles at any time, you can go to him. Why? Because you know he's not doing anything.

. . .

Our guest of honor is the kind of a guy you want to have working at your side. If the boss drops in unexpectedly you'll always look good by comparison.

. . .

I worked with our guest of honor for many years. And I'll say this, through thick and thin, happy and sad, good times and bad, he'll always be there for you. You know he's not going to get promoted.

. . .

I've recommended our guest of honor for jobs and promotions. In fact, the first day he walked into the office I turned to the boss and said, "Get him."

. . .

Our guest of honor is a good guy to have in the office because he's good for a lot of laughs. Of course, most of them are behind his back. . . .

. . .

As a coworker our guest of honor is unique. There's only one of him which is good because that's all our office can afford to carry.

. . .

Our guest of honor is not only my coworker, but I'd also say he's my best friend. Which should give you an idea of how lousy my social life has been.

. . .

Our guest of honor and I have been together through thick and thin
. . . but enough about both of our waistlines. . . .

A HARD WORKER

Every morning I get up and look through the *Forbes* list of the richest
people in America. If I'm not there, I go to work.
—*Robert Orben*

He's a self-made man . . . the living proof of the horrors of unskilled
labor.   —*Ed Wynn*

He's always got his foot to the pedal, his shoulder to the wheel, his
nose to the grindstone. How he gets any work done in that position,
I'll never know.

· · ·

Many times I've seen our guest of honor at work at the office even
when he was sick. I assume he was sick. I'd hate to think anyone
could look that bad when he was well.

· · ·

I'll say this for our guest of honor: he pulls his own weight, which for
him is a considerable amount of work.

· · ·

What makes him happy is to have a demanding, challenging project
on his desk. It makes the rest of us happy, too, because it keeps him
out of our hair.

· · ·

I told our guest of honor once that "all work and no play make Jack
a dull boy." So now, he and Jack hang around together.

· · ·

40

He's very ambitious. Someone asked him once, "What do you want?" He said honestly, "I want your job." Unfortunately, he was speaking to the janitor at the time.

. . .

Our guest of honor is attracted to work like a bee is to honey, which is annoying to the rest of us because the buzzing keeps us awake all day.

. . . it could also explain why he refers to the rest of us as "drones."

. . .

Our guest of honor is not happy unless he's working. If you don't believe me, take a look at him tonight.

. . .

He's the hardest worker I've ever seen in all my years at my desk. It might also explain why I've been at the same desk all these years.

. . .

Our guest of honor came into our office and worked harder than the rest of us and will probably move ahead of the rest of us. But that's not all. There are many other reasons why we don't like him.

. . .

Our guest of honor works so hard that he makes the rest of us work harder, too. In fact, he works right through lunch. Well, why not? He can't get any of us to eat with him.

NOT A HARD WORKER

The man with the best job in the country is the Vice-President. All he has to do is get up every morning and say, "How's the President?"
—*Will Rogers*

I was a lousy accountant. I always figured that if you came within eight bucks of what you needed you were doing okay. I made up the difference out of my own pocket. —*Bob Newhart*

He has a problem with his job. He doesn't do anything; so, he never knows when he's finished. —*Milton Berle*

There's no limit to the amount of work a man can do, provided, of course, that it isn't the work he's supposed to be doing at that moment. —*Robert Benchley*

The pencil sharpener is about as far as I have ever got in operating a complicated piece of machinery with any success.
—*Robert Benchley*

Hard work never killed anybody, but why take a chance?
—*Charlie McCarthy*

You know the old saying: If you want something done, give it to a busy man. Well, if you don't want something done, give it to our guest of honor.

. . .

He knows he's not a hard worker. Every payday he comes to work wearing a ski mask.

. . .

He has a sign over his desk that reads, "Thank you for not working."

. . .

Our guest of honor is very, very good at not doing any work. I went with him to the zoo one day. And when we got to the sloths' cage, they all came up and asked for his autograph.

. . .

If our guest of honor left our office it would take three workers to replace him. One to do his job and two to finish up the work he hasn't completed yet.

. . .

He was given a job and the first question he asked was "When do you need this done?" The boss said, "I don't need it done. That's why I gave it to you."

. . .

Our guest of honor has very simple work demands. All he needs is a project to work on and an office that sleeps one.

. . .

At work, our guest of honor keeps his nose to the grindstone and his shoulder to the wheel. The strange thing is, he can sleep in that position.

. . .

His out-basket caught fire once and he didn't discover it for four months.

Now he doesn't even have one. He's such a slow worker that the two baskets on his desk are marked "In" and "Still In."

. . .

Our guest of honor is the only guy I've ever worked with who, when he takes a two-week vacation, his productivity doesn't drop.

. . .

Our guest of honor considers himself a meticulous worker. He does nothing, but he does it without mistakes.

When Mohammed Ali was born, he was a six-pound mouth.
—*Bob Hope*

Jessel likes after-dinner speaking so much, he starts a speech at the mere sight of bread crumbs. —*Fred Allen*

I finally found out why talk is cheap. There's more supply than demand. —*Joey Adams*

Our guest of honor is an eloquent conversationalist, which means when he talks, everybody listens . . . but nobody knows what he's talking about.

. . .

I asked him. I said, "Don't you agree it's wrong to use a big, complex word when a simple one will do?" He said, "Indubitably."

. . .

Our guest of honor loves to talk. Even when he has nothing to say, he usually says it.

. . .

He has such a big vocabulary I can't really converse with him. The best I can do is nod in all the right places.

. . .

He has such a sophisticated vocabulary he makes William F. Buckley sound like Beavis and Butthead.

. . .

Our guest of honor loves to talk. When you ask him, "How are you doing?" he actually tells you.

. . .

He was born with a silver spoon in his mouth, but he took it out right away because he wanted to say something.

. . .

His parents still remember their first words after he was born: "Shut up."

. . .

Our guest of honor has a very powerful voice. He can call you on the telephone without even using the telephone.

. . .

His telephone voice is so loud, you can hang up on him without losing volume.

. . .

He has a very loud voice. He once called a group of us into his office, and every one went in—even people who weren't at work that day.

. . .

He yelled at me once and it took three weeks for my shoes to stop vibrating.

A PARTY GUY

Our guest of honor is a real party guy. You should see him at a convention . . . because chances are he can't see you.

. . .

Our guest of honor passed out at a party we had not too long ago. So we brought him to . . . then we brought him two more and he was fine.

. . .

Our guest of honor loves a good party. In fact, he loves it so much he often turns it into a *bad* party.

. . .

He loves parties. His middle name is RSVP.

. . .

Our guest of honor loves a good party. And if he has a good time at an affair, the next day we tell him about it.

. . .

His philosophy is "eat, drink, and be merry because the next party may not be for a whole week."

. . .

At one convention he woke up in his hotel room, and his clothes were strewn all over the floor. And he was still in them.

. . .

Our guest of honor likes to have a good time because, he says, life is too short. Of course it's short when you only remember about half of it.

. . .

Our guest of honor says he enjoys parties because he's full of life. I've seen him at some parties where that's not all he was full of.

. . .

Our guest of honor likes to have a good time with good friends. "Although," he says, "sometimes with bad friends you can have an even better time."

. . .

Our guest of honor says he can have a party with just himself and one good friend. In fact, he could have a great party without the one good friend, but then how would he get home?

. . .

I asked his wife earlier if he ever goes to sleep early. She said that he often goes to sleep early—about 50 feet before he reaches the front door.

A TOAST

ON THIS SPECIAL OCCASION

25 Years with the Company

Promotion

Leaving the Company

I drink to your 25 years with the company. It's amazing how time flies when you're forced to share an office with someone.

A toast: May you sit on the tack of success and rise quickly.

I toast your moving on to bigger and better things. We hated to lose you to another company, but it was the only way we could get rid of you.

25 YEARS WITH THE COMPANY

Our guest of honor is celebrating his 25th anniversary with the company tonight. So many years, so little accomplished.

. . .

Our guest of honor serving 25 years here makes us proud of ourselves. Not many companies could have endured that so graciously.

. . .

Twenty-five years is a long time. Those of us who have worked with our guest of honor know that.

. . .

I asked our guest of honor, "How do you feel about reaching the 25-year mark?" He said, "I feel great. Next I'm going for the quarter century."

Everyone understood that joke except the group from Accounting.

. . .

Let me give this audience an idea of what 25 years is: Count all your fingers on both hands. Now do it again. Then count the fingers on just one hand.

. . . For many of you that will come to 25.
. . . If it doesn't, have a friend count them for you.

. . .

Our guest of honor reported to this company 25 years ago—bright, eager, wet behind the ears. He's dried up since.

... behind the ears and a few other places.

• • •

I think our boss summed up this evening best when he said about our guest of honor, "Twenty-fifth anniversary? I thought I fired him years ago."

PROMOTION

You can sum up his success in one word, *lucky*.   —*Joey Adams*

I don't deserve this award, but I have arthritis and I don't deserve that either.   —*Jack Benny*

Our guest of honor has been promoted. That's great. It means there's hope for all of us.

• • •

Congratulations on your promotion. It couldn't have happened to a nicer person. A lot more deserving maybe, but none nicer.

• • •

The Peter Principle says that workers are promoted until they reach their level of incompetence. This promotion disproves that. Our guest of honor reached that level several promotions ago.

• • •

Why did our guest of honor get this promotion? Because he deserves it. The rest of us have to keep telling ourselves that.

• • •

Our guest of honor started in the company as a nothing, and look at him now—a nothing with a fancy title.

. . .

What's amazing is that our guest of honor got this promotion so early—many, many years before he deserved it.

. . .

With this promotion, many of us will now be working for our guest of honor. The rest of us will continue to work against him.

. . .

I've been a close friend of our guest of honor for many years. Now that he's gotten this promotion I realize that I never really cared for him.

. . .

I'll say this about our guest of honor: this promotion hasn't gone to his head. I've worked with him for many years, and I can honestly say that not much has gone to his head.

. . .

Even though I thought I might get this promotion, I was hoping our guest of honor would get it. In fact, I hope he gets everything that's coming to him.

. . .

I must tell you that I came here tonight a little upset that I didn't get this promotion. But since I've let the air out of his tires in the parking lot, I feel much better.

. . .

So, our guest of honor has been promoted. I'll tell you how I feel about that. He's now just one other person I'll have to step over on my way to the top.

50

LEAVING THE COMPANY

He's the kind of guy who can brighten a room by leaving it.
—*Milton Berle*

Our guest of honor is leaving the company for something better, which has upset management. They didn't want the rest of us to know there was anything better.

. . .

Our guest of honor is leaving the company. We hated to lose him, but it was either that or pay him more money.

. . .

I cautioned our guest of honor to be careful about leaving the company. I reminded him the grass is always greener. And he told me, "It's not only greener, but I'm getting more of it."

. . .

Why is our guest of honor leaving the company? Well, he's following the advice of the great philosopher Yogi Berra, who said, "Whenever you come to a fork in the road, take it."

. . .

To me, going-away parties are sad—because they're always for somebody else.

. . .

Our guest of honor decided to stop working here. That was years ago. Now he's decided to leave the company.

. . . he's going to start not working somewhere else.

. . .

Our guest of honor is moving on to bigger and better things. At least, that's the story he bought.

. . .

I asked our guest of honor why he was leaving us. He said, "Like the three little pigs in the story, I'm going out to make my way in the world." It's comforting to know he's leaving with good, solid role models.

. . .

We wish our guest of honor well. But we want him to know that if he ever wants to return, we'll be here for him . . . because most of us can't get a better job like he can.

. . .

In sports, when an honored player leaves, they retire his jersey. We're going to do the next best thing. We're going to retire his desk chair.

. . . the wheels on it don't work anyway.

. . . come to think of it, that may be why he's leaving.

CONGRATULATIONS ON YOUR

RETIREMENT

Losing a Coworker

Around the House

Travel

Fishing

Golf

Gardening

A toast to your retirement:
    Remember when you have nothing to do,
    That no one does that better than you.

To your retirement:
    Gardening, reading, golf, and fishing,
    May you lead the life for which we've all been wishing.

To your retirement:
    Here's to doing nothing at all.
    Relax, enjoy, and just have a ball.

    When you're sitting at home with nothing to do,
    Think of us still at work. We're doing that too.

LOSING A COWORKER

I went to the doctor last week. He told me to take a hot bath before retiring. That's ridiculous. It'll be years before I retire.
                                    —*Henny Youngman*

May your retirement plan be supervised by Jimmy Hoffa.
                                    —*Steve Allen*

Retirement at sixty-five is ridiculous. When I was sixty-five, I still had pimples.   —*George Burns*

Our guest of honor is retiring. We won't see his smiling face around the office, listen to his pleasant laugh, or have him to chip in to solve a problem. On the other hand, I'd say now is a great time to buy stock in the company.

                         • • •

From what I can tell, our guest of honor retired from work several years ago. He's just now letting the company in on it.

                         • • •

Retirement: that's nature's way of telling you you're not getting any more paychecks.

· · ·

I asked our retiree how long he's worked at this company. He said, "Oh, about half the years I've been here."

· · ·

To all of our guest of honor's fellow employees, I say look at it this way: you're not losing a coworker; you're gaining a desk to rifle.

· · ·

I asked our guest of honor, "What goes through your mind as you're about to retire?" He said, "Absolutely nothing. I don't want to start using my mind until I officially leave the company."

· · ·

Retirement can be a happy time, a pleasant time, a joyous time, unless you're married to the retiree.

· · ·

At the workplace I don't know what we'll do without our guest of honor. But you may have noticed, a lot of us didn't know what we were doing while he was there, either.

· · ·

It's sad when you leave the workplace and go home, but look on the bright side. Chances are you'll get a better parking spot there.

· · ·

Retirement is when you go home from work one day and never have to come back. The closest I can come to understanding that concept is one time, as a young lad, my father took me aside and left me there.

· · ·

I knew one gentleman who had a very active and worthwhile retirement. I ran into him and his wife at a reunion once and I said to her, "How's your husband doing since he retired three years ago?" And she said, "He did?"

· · ·

Retirement does not mean that the employee is no longer wanted or needed by the company. In this case, it happens to be true, but . . .

AROUND THE HOUSE

I'm an ordinary sort of fellow: 42 around the chest, 42 around the waist, 96 around the golf course, and a nuisance around the house.
—*Groucho Marx*

The trouble with not working is the minute you wake up in the morning, you're on the job. —*Slappy White*

Our guest of honor says he's going to enjoy just staying around the house. That's good because he deserves the best. I just feel sorry for his spouse because she deserves better.

. . .

His wife's a little worried, but our guest of honor says, "Don't worry about me. I'll find things to do around the house." She says, "That's what I'm worried about."

. . .

His wife said she may find him part-time work. He says, "Why? I don't mind hanging around the house." She said, "I do."

. . .

Our guest of honor told the boss he plans to become a gentleman of leisure. And the boss said, "Become?"

. . .

He told me in retirement he plans to do absolutely nothing. I said, "How long can you do that?" He said, "Until I run out of things to do."

. . .

I think our guest of honor will be good at doing nothing around the house because when we had nothing to do at the office, we generally assigned it to him.

. . .

You may wonder how a person can be happy just doing nothing. Well, in our guest of honor's case, it's from years and years of practice.

. . .

His wife told me, "For the first week he's home I'll get him anything he wants. The second week I'll get him a job."

. . .

His wife said she'll be glad to have him home. She said, "For years he's been coming home and asking me what I did all day. Now he can stay home and watch me do it."

. . .

I think our guest of honor will be good at staying home and doing nothing. He almost had it down pat while he worked next to me.

. . .

I think our guest of honor will enjoy retirement. When you get up in the morning you've got nothing to do and all day to do it in.

. . . and I'll bet he'll still have trouble getting it done in time.

TRAVEL

I took the vacation I wanted all my life. I packed Alice and the kids and all the luggage in our station wagon and headed it right straight to Canada. Then I went to Las Vegas and had a ball.

—*George Gobel*

If you like to travel to out-of-the-way places where few people go, let your wife read the map. —*Norm Crosby*

When you look like your passport photo, it's time to go home.
—*Erma Bombeck*

I travel a lot. You know, I've been to almost as many places as my luggage has. —*Bob Hope*

Our guest of honor says he plans to go places now that he's retired. That's good because he certainly didn't go places while he worked here.

. . .

You can tell from looking at our guest of honor that he's a traveling man. He must be. Practically everyone he meets tells him where to go.

. . .

Puerto Vallarta, Mazatlán, Nairobi. Now that our guest of honor has the time, he plans to learn how to spell those places.

. . .

Our guest of honor says that now that he's retired there'll be no grass growing under his feet. That either means he's going to travel or he plans to do his own gardening.

. . .

He's going to visit the quiet, peaceful places of the world like Hawaii, Bermuda, the Bahamas. That makes sense. If he wanted to visit trouble spots he could just continue working here.

. . .

Our guest of honor says he plans to live out of a suitcase from now on. That either means he's going to travel or he has to sell his house to augment his pension checks.

. . .

I asked our guest of honor where he was going to travel—USA? UK? He said, "ANH." I said, "Where's ANH?" He said, "Anyplace not here."

. . .

Our guest of honor said he's going to be busy because he's got places to go and people to see. Of course, while he worked here he had things to do, but that never kept him very busy.

. . .

He plans to sit on a beach chair, just doing nothing. That's quite a change after years and years of sitting at a desk chair just doing nothing.

. . .

Our guest of honor is not a very sophisticated traveler. He looks forward to boarding an airplane for the food.

. . .

He's built for travel, you know. He has a seat bottom that can be used as a flotation device.

. . .

Our guest of honor said he plans to travel like the wind, which is typical of him—to use the cheapest mode of transportation.

FISHING

My husband is one of those fishermen who wears those boots that extend up to the armpits so that when the water pours in, you are assured of drowning instantly. —*Erma Bombeck*

Our guest of honor says he is an incurable fisherman . . . unless, of course, he's lying about that, too.

. . .

Our guest of honor says he always catches his limit. I said, "How do you manage that?" He said, "Easy. I go where there's no fishing allowed."

. . .

Our guest of honor says that fishing is the most relaxing activity in the world. Those of us who have watched him at work find that hard to believe.

. . .

I asked him, "What's the hardest fish to catch?" He said, "One that keeps its mouth shut."

. . . he said that knowing I would be a speaker here tonight.

. . .

Our guest of honor said he enjoys fishing because it's a mental game. He likes to outsmart his prey. You have to admire a man who likes to prove he's smarter than a wall-eyed pike.

. . . some of the time.

. . .

I spend a lot of time fishing myself, but it's generally in conjunction with my golf game.

. . .

He said he generally throws the fish back. I said, "Why do you do that?" He said, "If you catch a 3-pound fish and take it home, it's a 3-pound fish. If you throw it back, when you get home it's a 5-pound fish."

. . .

I asked our guest of honor, "Where do you go to do most of your fishing?" He said, "Generally, near water."

. . .

I said, "Is anyone else in your family a fisherman?" He said, "No. Although several of them think they are."

. . .

Our guest of honor told me that to him fishing was the greatest sporting contest in the world. I asked why. He said, "Name one other sport where the loser is so delicious."

GOLF

Golf is a good walk spoiled.

—*Mark Twain*

Every time Jerry Ford plays golf, he gathers a big crowd. You know how people gather at the scene of an accident.　　　—*Bob Hope*

I found something that can take five points off your golf game—an eraser.　　　—*Joey Adams*

If you watch a game, it's fun. If you play it, it's recreation. If you work at it, it's golf.　　　—*Bob Hope*

I play in the low 80's. If it's any hotter than that, I won't play.

—*Joe E. Lewis*

Knowing our guest of honor, he'll probably go for several swims each day. Either that or he'll have to buy a new golf ball.

. . .

Our guest of honor likes to be alone in the woods, go places where few have gone before, and face challenges that are seemingly impossible. Unfortunately, he does all of this in a golf cart.

. . .

Our guest of honor will have a lot more time for golf—which is probably the only thing that will improve his swing.

. . .

One of his golfing goals is to shoot his age. And I hope he does it, too. I hope he's still playing golf when he's well over 100.

. . .

As one of his retirement gifts, we wanted to get him something he could use playing golf. But I understand he already has a calculator.

. . . some of those who have played with him suggested a lie detector.

. . .

Our guest of honor plays golf religiously. That means anytime he makes a good shot, it's considered a miracle.

. . .

He hits the ball all over the place. When he rents a golf cart, it has to be four-wheel drive.

. . .

Our guest of honor has fun playing golf. He says a great shot in golf is like your weekly salary. You don't have to earn it to enjoy it.

. . .

Our guest of honor is not a very good golfer. He's the guy who put the "P–U" in *Putt*.

. . .

Our guest of honor is going to enjoy golf in his retirement. I asked him earlier what his golf handicap was. He said, "Having to work for a living."

. . .

Our guest of honor has been trying to learn golf for a long time, but he confessed to me tonight that he's not very good at it. I said, "What kind of clubs do you use?" He said, "Clubs?"

GARDENING

Our guest of honor enjoys gardening, which has helped his career at work. He's used to spending a lot of time on his knees.

. . . and working around fertilizer.

. . .

He'll do a lot of gardening during his retirement. He says, "I plan to keep on gardening until the snails can outrun me."

. . .

Our guest of honor told me he plans to spend a lot of time in his garden. I don't know if that means he's going to work there or if his wife's going to take him outside and plant him.

. . .

Our guest of honor told me, "I'll be tossing fertilizer around and pruning all the dead wood I can find." It'll be just like he's back in management.

. . .

He said, "I like to work with dirt." I don't know what that says about those of us who have shared an office with him these past several years. . . .

. . .

I think our guest of honor will be very effective at gardening. I've worked with him many years and I know I wouldn't want to disagree with him while he had a Weedwacker in his hands.

. . .

He spends a lot of time on his hands and knees on the front lawn. We have a lot of people here who do that, but it's generally after one of these parties.

. . .

Our guest of honor says he loves to dig in the soil and get his hands dirty. I just mention that so those of you who shook hands with him earlier may want to wash up before dinner.

. . .

I think our guest of honor would be good at spreading fertilizer. Those of you who have heard him speak can probably vouch for that.

. . .

I said to our guest of honor, "When I see you a few months from now, may I ask 'How does your garden grow?' " He said, "Sure, if you'd like to get hit across the bridge of your nose with a hoe."

. . .

I said, "When I drive by your house in a few months will I see rows and rows of petunias, daffodils, and marigolds?" He said, "I hope not. I planted tomatoes."

WE ARE PLEASED TO INVITE YOU TO OUR

WEDDING ANNIVERSARY

So Many Years Together

Forgetting Anniversaries

Anniversary Gifts

Here's a toast to the many good times you've enjoyed together . . . and to the one or two that you just tolerated.

A toast to your anniversary. You've had many good years together, either that or one helluva good prenuptial agreement.

Here's to your love that has survived many years and is all the stronger for it.

A toast to your anniversary and the love that has held you together these many years:
When times are good, it's easy, brother.
When times are tough is when you need one another.

It's nice to see such a happily married couple after so many years, because here's what "they" say about marriage:

It's better to have loved and lost than to have loved and married.
—*Sammy Shore*

Your wife is like TV. It's home and it's free.   —*Slappy White*

Husbands are like fires. They go out if unattended.
—*Zsa Zsa Gabor*

My wife has a nice even disposition—miserable all the time.
—*Henny Youngman*

Twenty years ago, I married for richer, for poorer, for better, for worse. Fang's so lazy he hasn't been any of those things.
—*Phyllis Diller*

After all these years of marriage, I get the impression I married a knickknack. —*Phyllis Diller*

Many years ago, our guests of honor set sail on the sea of matrimony. And tonight, despite a few barnacles, they're still afloat.

. . .

Our guests of honor are celebrating their wedding anniversary tonight. I asked how many years it's been and they both answered, "Enough."

. . .

Our guests of honor told me that the secret of their longevity is that they never go to sleep angry at one another. Over their so many years of marriage, they figure they've lost about 8 years of sleep.

. . .

They've been together a long time. That's the nice thing about a big wedding. You feel obligated to stay together until it's paid for.

. . .

The groom told me he has the same thoughts tonight that he did on his wedding night. "Let's eat the cake; I'm starving."

. . .

She said, "It's our silver [golden] wedding anniversary. Let's go out and have an elegant, expensive, romantic dinner." He said, "OK, but I hope you're not going to expect this every 25 [50] years."

. . .

A couple of the groom's old girlfriends are here. At his age, what other kind of girlfriends would he have?

. . .

These two people were made for one another. Who else would have them?

. . .

It's nice to see a couple that's been married this long look so happy together. They're either doing something right or they have no idea that they're doing something wrong.

. . .

The groom told me that the suit he wore at his wedding fits him perfectly today. That gives you an idea how baggy it must have been on the day he was married.

. . .

The groom told me he can still get into his wedding suit—about halfway.

. . .

I asked the bride tonight, "Is he still the man you married?" She said, "He's almost double that."

. . .

This couple should stay married a long time. The bride told me she married him for better, for worse, for richer, for poorer. And she's determined to stay with him till things start getting better and richer.

. . .

Their wedding anniversary is proof that there is someone in this world for everybody. I just feel sorry for her that she had to get *him*.

. . . but somebody had to.

. . . just to take him out of circulation.

. . . and to make things safer for the rest of us.

. . .

I said to someone earlier tonight, "They still make a beautiful couple, don't they?" He said, "Couple of what?"

. . .

Our guests of honor have been married quite a while. There's some controversy over the number of years. Apparently, it's been longer for her than it has for him.

. . .

They've been married a long time and it's nice to know that their love has grown even more than his waistline.

FORGETTING ANNIVERSARIES

I asked our guest of honor how many anniversaries he's forgotten over the years. He said, "I forget."

. . .

I have a friend who was married on February 29th so that he would only forget to buy an anniversary gift every four years.

. . .

Over the years he's forgotten a few anniversary gifts, but she gets even. She's forgotten to tell him which mushrooms are store-bought and which ones she picked herself.

. . .

I have a friend who tells me her husband has no idea what day they were married on. I said, "Oh, that's too bad." She said, "No, that's good. I can get an anniversary gift from him anytime I want one."

. . .

I asked our guest of honor if he was the kind to forget his anniversaries. He said, "Never more than once in the same year."

. . .

I spoke to our guest of honor earlier. I said, "You know what my mother used to say about people like you? 'You'd forget your head if it weren't screwed on.' " You know, he actually checked.

. . .

She told me that his forgetfulness helps keep the marriage going. Every time she's a little grumpy, he buys her flowers, takes her out to dinner, and wishes her a happy anniversary.

. . .

I asked him tonight, "When were you married?" He said, "I think it was in another life."

. . .

It seems only the men forget anniversaries. I asked the bride tonight and she told me, "I've never forgotten the day we were married. And heaven knows, there have been times when I've tried."

. . .

It is the secret to a long marriage. She told me tonight, she's going to keep him until he remembers an anniversary.

. . .

But he does buy lovely anniversary gifts, she told me. Fine china, elegant silverware, linen napkins. He once took her to a restaurant that uses those.

. . .

She has never forgotten an anniversary. As she told me, "If you were married to him, would you forget the day it happened?"

For our anniversary my wife wanted to go someplace she's never been before. So I took her to the kitchen.   —*Henny Youngman*

I don't know what to get my wife for our anniversary anymore. First she wanted a mink. I got her a mink. Then she wanted a silver fox. I got her a silver fox. It was ridiculous. The house was full of animals.
     —*Henny Youngman*

For our anniversary, my wife wanted a white mink coat. I told her I'd buy her a white mink coat when a man walked on the moon. My luck.   —*Henny Youngman*

70

She told me she has trouble getting him an anniversary gift. You know the dilemma: what do you get for a man who has everything? Her problem is: what do you get for the man who understands nothing?

. . .

I asked her what she got her husband for their anniversary. She said, "Nothing. It's his favorite pastime."

. . .

You know there are golf shops, tennis shops, and so on. I suggested she go to a store that specializes in his favorite activity. So she got him a gift certificate from Naps-R-Us.

. . .

They already exchanged anniversary gifts. He gave her a piece of cheap jewelry; she gave him a piece of her mind.

. . .

For their anniversary he bought something for the house—a round of drinks.

. . .

She said she wanted something that a woman can use forever. He bought her a diet book.

. . .

For her anniversary gift to him, she cooked his favorite meal. For his anniversary gift to her, he ate it.

. . .

He said, "I'd like to have something that goes with my favorite sports coat." So she got him a clown's nose.

. . .

For this anniversary they decided to get themselves something that they've both wanted since 1972. They bought a 1972 Cadillac.

. . .

When they were discussing anniversary gifts, he said, "I've given you my undying love and devotion. What more could you want?" She came back with a list about 8 feet long.

. . .

She told a friend, "I think I'll get something that's useful around the house." He overheard and thought she was seeing another man.

. . .

She asked if it was all right if she took the anniversary gift he gave her back to the store. She thought she could exchange it and maybe use the refund as a down payment on something worthwhile.

A PHOTO ALBUM OF MEMORIES FOR YOUR

MARRIAGE

Wedding

Honeymoon

Marriage Lasts Forever

Here's to your wedding. May you always love each other a little bit more than yesterday but not quite as much as tomorrow.

A toast: May the bride and groom have as much happiness as I've had on several occasions. —*George Jessel*

To your wedding: Love not only makes the world go 'round, but it also makes the trip worthwhile.

To your wedding: May your love for each other grow as surely as your waistlines will.

My wife and I were happy for twenty years. Then we met.
—*Rodney Dangerfield*

My wife's an earth sign. I'm a water sign. Together we make mud.
—*Rodney Dangerfield*

We sleep in separate rooms, we have dinner apart, we take separate vacations. We're doing everything we can to keep our marriage together. —*Henny Youngman*

The first part of our marriage was very happy. But then, on the way back from the ceremony . . . —*Henny Youngman*

My parents want me to get married. They don't care who anymore, as long as he doesn't have a pierced ear, that's all they care about. I think men who have a pierced ear are better prepared for marriage. They've experienced pain and bought jewelry. —*Rita Rudner*

I found out after I got married that the husband's closet never comes with the apartment. *—Rodney Dangerfield*

Politics doesn't make strange bedfellows, marriage does. *—Groucho Marx*

Since I've been married, I don't have to worry about bad breath. I never get a chance to open my mouth. *—Rodney Dangerfield*

If you want to read a book on love and marriage you've got to buy two separate books. *—Alan King*

Some stuff does bother me about being married . . . like having a husband. *—Roseanne Barr*

He tricked me into marrying him. He told me I was pregnant. *—Carol Leifer*

A couple is driving to Miami Beach in a brand-new car. As they're driving, he puts his hand on her knee. She says, "We're married now, you can go a little farther." So he went to Fort Lauderdale. *—Henny Youngman*

'Tis more blessed to give than receive; for example, wedding gifts. *—H. L. Mencken*

I just found out why they rope off the aisles at a wedding. It's so the groom can't get away. *—Joey Adams*

I went to a wedding . . . I couldn't believe the groom was married in rented shoes. You're making a commitment for a lifetime, and your shoes have to be back by 5:30. *—Jerry Seinfeld*

I was the best man at the wedding. If I'm the best man, why is she marrying him? *—Jerry Seinfeld*

When a woman marries again it is because she detested her first husband. When a man marries again, it is because he adored his first wife. Women try their luck; men risk theirs. *—Oscar Wilde*

I wore a white dress on my wedding day . . . it had a big black hem.
—*Joan Rivers*

I was one of the few brides who ever got a request from the congregation to keep the veil on.
—*Phyllis Diller*

So, you two are going to tie the knot? Knowing him as well as I do, I'd suggest you tie it very tight.

. . .

You are going to accept him for richer, for poorer, for better, for worse. Take a good look at him and I think you can rule out a couple of those right from the start.

. . .

She has been looking for a good man for some time. And even though she is marrying *him*, I hope she doesn't abandon the search.

. . .

She's been going with him for quite a while, which is a good sign that she certainly knows how to handle children.

. . .

We're all so happy that you're having a big wedding. We're always happy when it means we get a free meal and a piece of cake.

. . .

I should warn you that he's very cheap. In fact, when you throw the bouquet, he may try to catch it.

. . . and sell it back to you.

. . .

I must say you do make a perfect couple . . . except for him.

. . .

He has so many faults, his nickname is San Andreas.

. . .

Let's put it this way, . . . I've known him a lot longer than you have, and I never offered to marry him.

. . . well, maybe I did, but that was at the bachelor party.

. . .

Soon you two will become one, which is about how many can survive on his salary.

. . . almost.

. . .

And of course, being married now entitles you to do mother-in-law jokes, like these:

The only reason my mother-in-law wasn't on Noah's Ark was because they couldn't find another animal that looked like her.
—*Phyllis Diller*

The day I got married. What a day that was, when they said, "Speak now or forever hold your peace." Her family formed a double line.
—*Rodney Dangerfield*

I said to my mother-in-law, "My house is your house." So, she sold it. —*Henny Youngman*

I'm just back from a pleasure trip. I took my mother-in-law to the airport. —*Henny Youngman*

My mother-in-law had plastic surgery. She had a little work done on her nose . . . they put it in the middle of her face. —*Redd Foxx*

My mother-in-law has such a big mouth. When she smiles, there's lipstick on her ears. —*Redd Foxx*

HONEYMOON

A loser is a guy who goes on a honeymoon, and the motel employees toss a welcome-back party for his wife. —*Charlie Manna*

We've been married for 50 years. Went back to the same hotel
where we got married, had the same suite of rooms. Only this time
I went into the bathroom and cried.   —*Henny Youngman*

On my honeymoon, Fang told me to unbutton my pajamas, and I
wasn't wearing any.   —*Phyllis Diller*

The cooing stops with the honeymoon; the billing goes on forever.
                                             —*Milton Berle*

After we made love he took a piece of chalk and made an outline of
my body.   —*Joan Rivers*

Romeo and Juliet got married. They spent one night together and
the next day he committed suicide. Then she committed suicide. I'm
trying to figure what went on in that bedroom.   —*Alan King*

We don't know where they're going on their honeymoon. And probably when they get back, they won't remember where they've been.

• • •

We all know what a honeymoon is. It's a way of getting far away
while someone else pays for the wedding.

• • •

Enjoy this, your first honeymoon. If you're like the rest of us, you'll
never be able to afford a second one.

• • •

A honeymoon is when you go to a crowded resort so that you can
have some time alone.

• • •

The secret of a good marriage is to make the honeymoon last forever, although it's hard to make reservations for that long.

• • •

A honeymoon is a week or two of complete togetherness. For many
married couples, that's plenty.

• • •

78

I have a warning for you. You married each other for richer, for poorer. The poorer part comes when you get the bill for the honeymoon.

. . .

Remember this about your honeymoon. Two can live as cheaply as one, but not when you order room service.

. . .

You should try to make the honeymoon last forever ... and you pretty much can if you pay for it in installments.

. . .

The honeymoon should be the happiest time of your life. And even if it isn't, they still charge you for it as if it were.

. . .

A honeymoon is a time when you can get away and leave all your troubles behind, except if the person you married is one of those troubles.

. . .

We wanted to have this celebration for you before your wedding and your honeymoon. Let's be sure to do this again on your 25th anniversary.

MARRiAGE LASTS FOREVER

Anyone who thinks marriage is a fifty-fifty proposition doesn't understand either women or percentages. *—Henny Youngman*

Zsa Zsa Gabor has been married six times now; she's got rice marks on her face. *—Henny Youngman*

At least now he gives his wife something to live for: a divorce.
—*Henny Youngman*

Marriage is a great institution, but I'm not ready for an institution.
—*Mae West*

For the first four months of our marriage, I never took my wig off. Little did he know the hair he loved to touch he could take with him to the office.
—*Joan Rivers*

Last week I told my wife a man is like wine, he gets better with age. She locked me in the cellar.
—*Rodney Dangerfield*

Take a good look at the face of the mate you choose. You're going to wake up looking at that face for the rest of your life.

. . .

Marriage lasts forever. And those of us who are married will agree that at times it certainly seems that way.

. . .

Marriage is for a lifetime. Actually, it's for *two* lifetimes . . . served concurrently.

. . .

They really should hang a sign in all churches and wedding chapels that reads, "All decisions are final."

. . .

Our guests of honor should realize that when you purchase a marriage license it's a lifetime commitment. There should be no reason to save the receipt.

. . .

Marriage is forever . . . with time off for good behavior.

. . .

Matrimony is like getting a new car. Basically, you're buying your partner "as is."

And like it or not, you can get a lemon.

80

MANY HAPPY RETURNS ON YOUR

BIRTHDAY

Getting Older

Old Age

We drink a toast to you on your birthday. It was either that or get a couple of Boy Scouts to help you across the street.

. . .

We drink to you on your birthday. You're not getting older, you're getting better . . . or vice versa.

. . .

A toast to your birthday. Another year older, another day wiser.

GETTING OLDER

You know you're getting older when you stoop down to tie your shoes and wonder what else you can do while you're down there.
—*George Burns*

He's a man who just reached middle age for the third time.
—*Joe E. Lewis*

You know you've reached middle age when someone tells you to pull in your stomach and you just did.   —*Milton Berle*

I don't plan to grow old gracefully. I plan to have face-lifts until my ears meet.   —*Rita Rudner*

Middle age is when you've met so many people that every new person you meet reminds you of someone else.   —*Ogden Nash*

There's an old saying, "You're not getting older; you're getting better." I used to believe that saying until I met our guest of honor.

. . . he's getting wider.

. . .

I guess you know you're getting older when you start to hurt in places where a few years ago you didn't even know you had places.

. . .

You know you're getting older when the only parts of your body that don't hurt are the parts that have already fallen off.

. . .

You know you're getting older when your favorite pickup line is, "Do you come here often, and do you know CPR?"

. . .

Yep, you're only as young as you feel. And when you don't feel anything, you're old.

. . .

You know you're getting older when everybody starts telling you how young you look.

. . .

You know you're getting older when each time you want to stand up you have to think up a new sound to come out of your body.

. . .

You know you're getting older when one of your favorite hobbies is liniment.

. . .

You know you're getting older when even kids who aren't in the Boy Scouts start helping you across the street.

. . .

You know you're getting older when people start talking to you louder than they talk to other people. I SAY, WHEN PEOPLE START TALKING TO YOU LOUDER THAN THEY TALK TO OTHER PEOPLE.

. . .

You know you're getting older when all your favorite stories begin: "This was probably way before you were born, but . . ."

. . .

You know you're getting older when your favorite form of recreation is just staying in whatever position you're already in.

OLD AGE

He's so old that when he orders a three-minute egg, they ask for the money up front. —*Milton Berle*

You're never too old to become younger. —*Mae West*

I don't fear old age. I am just becoming more aware of the fact that the only people who said old age was beautiful were usually 23-year-olds. —*Erma Bombeck*

My grandmother is over eighty and still doesn't need glasses. Drinks right out of the bottle. —*Henny Youngman*

She was so old, when she went to school they didn't have history. —*Rodney Dangerfield*

I have my eighty-seventh birthday coming up and people ask what I'd most appreciate getting. I'll tell you: a paternity suit. —*George Burns*

No woman should ever be quite accurate about her age. It looks so calculating. —*Oscar Wilde*

The secret to staying young is to live honestly, eat slowly, and lie about your age. —*Lucille Ball*

One should never trust a woman who tells one her real age. A woman who would tell one that, would tell one anything. —*Oscar Wilde*

Old age is when your eyes start to go, but it doesn't really matter because whatever you read today you're going to forget tomorrow anyway.

. . .

The best way to keep looking young is to hang around with older people.

. . . if you can find any.

. . .

Old age is when gravity is more than a law; it's an adversary.

. . .

Old age is when you can say anything you want at any time because hardly anybody listens to you anyway.

. . .

The strange thing about senility is that anybody who knows he has it doesn't have it.

. . .

If you get old enough, you don't have to act your age, because nobody knows what that age should act like.

. . .

Sure, it's nice to outlive all your enemies, but then again, you've got no one to gloat over.

. . .

You can get away with a lot in your old age. You can do things you've been dying to do since you were a kid.

. . .

After a certain age, there's one thing you learn never to say: "How do I look?"

. . . someone just might tell you.

. . .

We always say of the deceased that "they've gone on to a better place." But deep down inside, we're glad to still be here.

CONGRATULATIONS ON YOUR

NEW BABY

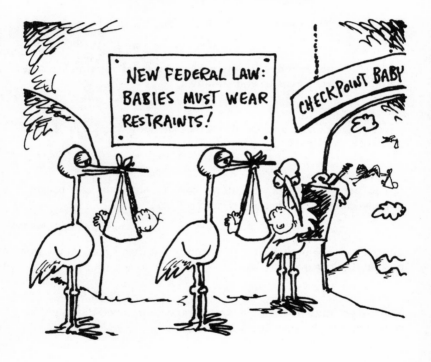

Having a Baby

Parenting

Here's a toast to your new baby . . . because nobody wants to give birth to an old baby.

A toast to your blessed event: For people your age, that means you're having a baby. For people my age, "blessed event" means you won the lottery.

A toast to your happiness: Soon the stork will be coming your way, followed shortly by the diaper service, the baby photographer, and probably an encyclopedia salesman or two.

HAVING A BABY

Did you hear the one about the expectant father who wanted to name the baby Oscar because it was his best performance of the year? —*Henny Youngman*

A little parenting advice: Don't call a baby-sitter who knows your children. She won't come. —*Phyllis Diller*

I once asked my father if things were bad for him during the Depression. He said the first six months were bad, then he got used to me. —*Rodney Dangerfield*

When I was pregnant, I told Fang the pains were three minutes apart. He used me to time the eggs. —*Phyllis Diller*

I was cesarean-born. You can't really tell. Although whenever I leave a house, I go out through a window. —*Steven Wright*

We delivered our child via natural childbirth. That's where it's believed that women can counteract the incredible pain of childbirth through breathing. That's like asking a man to tolerate a vasectomy by hyperventilating. —*Dennis Wolfberg*

I want to have children, but my friends scare me. One of my friends told me she was in labor for thirty-six hours. I don't even want to do anything that feels good for thirty-six hours. —*Rita Rudner*

A woman came to ask the doctor if a woman should have children after thirty-five. I said thirty-five children is enough for any woman.
—*Gracie Allen*

I was born by C-section. This was the last time I had my mother's complete attention. —*Richard Jeni*

When my wife was about to give birth I said, "Honey, if it looks like you it would be great." She said, "If it looks like you, it'd be a miracle." —*Rodney Dangerfield*

A baby is an inestimable blessing and bother. —*Mark Twain*

I was an ugly baby. When my parents left me on a doorstep, they were arrested. Not for abandonment—for littering. —*Joan Rivers*

We haven't all the good fortune to be ladies. We have not all been generals, or poets, or statesmen, but when the toast works down to the babies we stand on common ground. We've all been babies.
—*Mark Twain*

Except that right side up is best, there is not much to learn about holding a baby. —*Heywood Broun*

The child had his mother's eyes, and his mother's nose, and his mother's mouth, which leaves his mother with a pretty blank expression. —*Robert Benchley*

My husband and I decided to explain the beautiful reproduction cycle to our kids through the animal kingdom. We bought two pairs of guppies and a small aquarium. We should have bought two pairs of guppies and a small reservoir. —*Erma Bombeck*

Congratulations on your blessed event. Take some advice from someone who's already been a parent. Get all your sleep in now.

. . .

Babies are the greatest pleasure in the whole world, until you've had them a month or two. Then a good night's sleep is.

. . .

Babies are a bundle of joy. It's just that seven or eight times a day you have to change the bundle.

. . .

Hospitals treat expectant fathers like vice-presidents. They put you in a room someplace and forget about you.

. . .

I told my wife, "I'd rather have the babies than do the grocery shopping." So we compromised. Now every time shopping day rolls around, I get morning sickness.

. . .

I want you to take a look at our couple right now. That's the way they're going to be for a long time after this baby arrives—wide awake.

. . .

When is the baby due? Well, as my grandmother used to say, "When the apple's ripe, it'll fall." Of course, if they go through all of this and wind up with an apple, it's going to be a terrible shock.

. . .

So you're going to have a child, huh? Plan ahead. You've only got sixteen more years to use the car whenever you want to.

. . .

I hope our guest of honor is smart enough to be a daddy. I asked him earlier if he wanted a boy or a girl. He said, "Yes."

. . .

Newborn babies are precious. When you get that hospital bill you'll realize they work out to about $750 a pound.

. . .

I'm sure you'll both enjoy this blessed event. Babies are cute and cuddly and precious. They're so much more fun than free time.

PaRenTinG

A little old lady was on a park bench. A neighbor admired her two little grandchildren and asked how old they were. The little old lady said: "The lawyer is four and the doctor is six." —*Alan King*

As parents my wife and I have one thing in common. We're both afraid of children. —*Bill Cosby*

My mother had a great deal of trouble with me, but I think she enjoyed it. —*Mark Twain*

Mothers mold the children's mind. Some of you have done well. There are a lot of moldy-minded kids around. —*Norm Crosby*

Parents were invented to make children happy by giving them something to ignore. —*Ogden Nash*

The height of parental maturity is, of course, to learn to live with your child as he is—even if he is just like you. —*Sam Levenson*

Babies on television never spit up on the Ultrasuede.
—*Erma Bombeck*

Ah, the pitter-patter of little feet in the house. There's nothing like having a midget for a butler. —*W. C. Fields*

I could now afford all the things I never had as a kid, if I didn't have kids. —*Robert Orben*

Kids! I can't make them disappear, but I do wear dark glasses in the house hoping they won't recognize me. —*Phyllis Diller*

Having a family is like having a bowling alley installed in your head.
—*Martin Mull*

Children have been known to take a few years off your life—like fifty or sixty.
—*George Burns*

The reason grandparents and grandchildren get along so well is that they have a common enemy.
—*Sam Levenson*

There are slight differences between mothers and grandmothers. Grandmothers say, "Stay in, it's cold outside." Mothers say, "Go out, it's good for you."
—*Erma Bombeck*

A grandfather is a man who can't understand how his idiot son had such brilliant children.
—*Milton Berle*

My grandmother was a very tough woman. She buried three husbands. Two of them were just napping.
—*Rita Rudner*

The only thing I ever said to my parents when I was a teenager was "Hang up. I got it."
—*Carol Leifer*

. . .

Parenting requires patience, endurance, forgiveness, understanding. And if the children aren't willing to do that, it's going to be tough.

. . .

No one can tell you how to be a good parent, except your children when they get to be teenagers.

. . .

You can take a test to see if you have the patience, flexibility, and endurance to be a good parent. You take this test when your child reaches the age of two.

. . .

I asked my mother what I should do to make sure that I raise my kids properly. She said, "I raised *you*. What do I know?"

. . .

You raise a child mostly by example. That's why to this day I still take a nap every day at two o'clock.

YOU ARE INVITED
TO BORROW THESE

INSULTS FOR ALL OCCASIONS

I drink to your charm, your beauty, and your brains—which gives you a rough idea of how hard up I am for a drink. —*Groucho Marx*

Let us toast the fools; but for them, the rest of us could not succeed.
—*Mark Twain*

I can't forget the first time I laid eyes on you . . . and don't think I haven't tried.
—*Henny Youngman*

You have a ready wit. Let me know when it's ready.
—*Henny Youngman*

I never forget a face, and in your case I'll remember both of them.
—*Henny Youngman*

There is a lot to say in her favor, but the other is more interesting.
—*Mark Twain*

You got a nice personality but not for a human being.
—*Jack E. Leonard*

His mother should have thrown him away and kept the stork.
—*Mae West*

I enjoyed talking to you. My mind needed a rest.
—*Henny Youngman*

What's on your mind, if you will allow the overstatement?
—*Fred Allen*

I never forget a face, but in your case I'll be glad to make an exception.
—*Groucho Marx*

Here's a toast that we may all learn to laugh at ourselves, because if we don't, someone else surely will.

. . .

Our guest of honor is a gem of a man. Of course, as you know, a gem is nothing more than a rock that got lucky.

. . .

Our guest of honor is a fine-looking gentleman. I'm sure most of us here wish that we could look that good when we get to be his age.

. . .

We have a rule at these affairs that if you can't say something nice about the guest of honor, don't say anything at all. This may be the first banquet done entirely in pantomime.

. . .

We have a rule at these affairs that if you can't say something nice about the guest of honor, don't say anything at all. So in conclusion . . .

. . .

I'd like to say that our guest of honor is probably the finest person I've ever met in my entire life. I'd like to say that, but I'd be laughed out of here if I did.

. . .

I'll tell you something about our guest of honor. Sometimes we say some nasty things at these roasts and the guest of honor's family gets annoyed. Tonight we said some nasty things about our guest of honor and his family just nodded in agreement.

. . .

All of us will agree that our guest of honor has a good head on his shoulders. Unfortunately, it's on his left shoulder instead of in the middle.

. . .

Our guest of honor is a very shy, reticent man. When we first told him about this affair, he said, "I don't think I'll be there." And we didn't care.

. . .

They don't make men like our guest of honor anymore. No, his sort went out of style years ago.

. . . he's like the Nehru jacket of personalities.

. . .

Our guest of honor is a self-made man. No professional would do the job.

Hilarious One·Liners

Contents

THE BEEP ON THE ROAD TO SUCCESS   339

MONEY   353

WORDS OF WISDOM   366

INTRODUCTION

Abraham Lincoln was sometimes criticized as a president who was too quick with a quip. He could answer a serious question with a laugh-getting response. He explained: "I often avoid a long and useless discussion by others or a laborious explanation on my part by [telling] a short story that illustrates my point of view."

To paraphrase the revered president, a good little joke cuts through all the baloney.

That's what a fresh, funny one-liner does. It's a concise statement that says an awful lot. It packs a wealth of meaning into a frugal few words. Along with its wisdom, it produces a chuckle.

One-liners are fun to read and fun to quote later.

This book contains many of our favorites on a variety of topics. Mark Twain got it right: "Grief can take care of itself, but to get the full value of joy, you must divide it with someone." The collection of gags in this book is our way of getting their full value of joy by sharing them with you. Enjoy.

Oh, and Abraham Lincoln added this about his joke-telling: "I do not seek applause . . . nor to amuse the people. I want to convince them." In other words, a good one-liner has a point to it, a valid lesson behind it. So, read, laugh, and maybe pick up an idea or two along the way. Have fun.

—Gene Perret with Terry Perret Martin

FUN & GAMES

Fun

Laughter

Games

Games People Play

Toys

Boomerangs

Football

Baseball

Hockey

Golf

Boxing

Fishing

There is no such thing as fun for the entire family.—*Jerry Seinfeld*

If you watch a game, it's fun. If you play at it, it's recreation.
If you work at it, it's golf.—*Bob Hope*

Want to have some fun? Send someone a telegram and on top put
"page 2."—*Henny Youngman*

Want to have some fun? Send someone a telegram saying,
"Ignore first telegram."—*Henny Youngman*

Good women are no fun. The only good woman I can recall was Betsy
Ross, and all she ever made was a flag. —*Mae West*

Did you ever hear someone say this: "It was more fun than a barrel of
monkeys." Did you ever *smell* a barrel of monkeys?—*Steve Bluestein*

Always try to keep a smile on your face because it looks silly on other
parts of your body.

I used to proclaim that laughter is the best medicine . . . until my family
doctor sued me for practicing without a license.

Let a smile be your umbrella, and see if you don't get a lot of strange
looks during the next thundershower.

We should have a lot of big belly laughs tonight because this audience is
certainly equipped for it.

Smile even when you're unhappy. That's because there's a good chance you'll make people who are happier than you are a little less happy.

It's easy for everyone to have at least one good belly laugh a day. All you need is a full-length mirror in the same room where you take your shower.

I adopted the philosophy of life: If it ain't fun, don't do it. The first person to lose money because of it was my dentist.

Try to keep a smile on your face and a melody in your heart. Once you master that, try patting your head and rubbing your belly at the same time.

You show me a man who can't take a joke, and I'll show you a man who should never wear Bermuda shorts in public.

One speaker told us a funny joke he heard. It was funny when he heard it, but not when he told it.

If you can't make it better, you can laugh at it.—*Erma Bombeck*

Want to have some fun?
Walk into an antique shop
and say, "What's new?"
        —*Henny Youngman*

It's bad to suppress laughter. It goes back down and spreads your hip.
—*Fred Allen*

An onion can make people cry, but there has never been a vegetable
invented to make them laugh.—*Will Rogers*

If I get big laughs, I'm a comedian. If I get small laughs, I'm a humorist.
If I get no laughs, I'm a singer.—*George Burns*

Laughter is the sensation of feeling good all over, and showing it, princi-
pally in one spot.—*Josh Billings*

When my Uncle Willie laughed, his belly shook like Jell-O. Come to
think of it, even when Uncle Willie sat still, his belly shook like Jell-O.

As one comedian said, "If my jokes can make just one person laugh this
evening, I'll probably be fired before tomorrow evening."

My Aunt Hattie had a loud, raucous laugh that she enjoyed for 57 years,
until a family of hyenas sued her for copyright infringement.

Remember that laughter spelled backwards is "rethgual." It means
absolutely nothing, but it just might cheer you up.

I love to hear laughter from an audience, because sometimes I don't know
where the punch lines are.

Laughter is good for your body, soul, and spirit. It makes the comedian feel a little better about himself, too.

Laugh and the world laughs with you. Stub your toe and the world laughs whether you do or not.

Aunt Louisa used to laugh like a cackling hen. Uncle Bert would have gotten rid of her, except he needed the eggs.

"Love makes the world go 'round," but laughter keeps us all from jumping off.

GAMES

I never got respect. I remember when I was a kid and played hide-and-seek . . . they wouldn't even look for me.—*Rodney Dangerfield*

I stayed up one night playing poker with Tarot cards. I got a full house and four people died.—*Steven Wright*

I bet on a horse ten to one. It didn't come in until half past five.
—*Henny Youngman*

No horse can go as fast as the money you bet on him.—*Nate Collier*

Race track: A place where windows clean people. —*Henny Youngman*

The horse I bet on was so late getting home, he tiptoed into the stable.
—*Henny Youngman*

Never play peek-a-boo with a child on a long plane trip. There's no end to the game. Finally I grabbed him by the bib and said, "Look. It's always gonna be me."—*Rita Rudner*

The only game I like to play is Old Maid—provided she's not too old.
—*Groucho Marx*

They love their gambling in Atlantic City. I saw
a guy putting a quarter in the parking meter. I said, "Are you crazy?"
He said, "Look at the odds—8 to 5."—*Bob Hope*

My horse finished so far back, the jockey had to run ahead of him with a
flashlight.—*Bob Hope*

I follow the horses. And the horses I follow, follow horses.—*Joe E. Lewis*

. . .

Gambling: That's throwing money away while other people cheer you on.

Casino gambling is strange. You put down five dollars. They spin the
wheel, take your money, and tell you what a good time you're having.

My brother was real good at playing hide-and-seek. He was so good at it
that we haven't seen him since 1952.

I didn't like to play hide-and-seek when I was young. My invisible playmate always won.

I never liked hide-and-seek. Not since the time I hid in the closet, and my
family moved.

I was never very good at sports. When I played in Little League, my own
father traded me to another team.
. . . for ten dollars and a child to be born later.

We used to play spin-the-bottle when I was a kid. A girl would spin the
bottle, and if the bottle pointed to you when it stopped, the girl could

either kiss you or give you a nickel. By the time I was 14, I owned my own home.

My best game as a kid was tiddlywinks until I had a career-ending injury.
. . . I sprained my wink finger.
. . . It could have been worse. I could have broken my tiddly.

My friend thought he was not gonna make it; then he started thinking positive. Now he's positive he's not gonna make it.—*Sammy Shore*

It's hard to be nice to some paranoid schizophrenic just because she lives in your body.—*Judy Tenuta*

Right now I'm having amnesia and déjà vu at the same time.
—*Steven Wright*

My boyfriend and I broke up. He wanted to get married, and I didn't want him to.—*Rita Rudner*

People today say they've got to "find themselves." My mother would have said to them, "If you'd put things away when you're done with them . . ."

If I ever told my father, "I'm trying to get my head on straight," he would have knocked it off for me.

A lot of people today play head games, but I don't. I don't want to buy a lot of expensive equipment.

Everybody is looking for equality today. They all want more of it than the next guy.

Greed is one of the seven deadly sins. I know a guy who's so greedy he has eight deadly sins.
. . . He had one custom-made.

Greed is silly. You come into this world with nothing, and you leave with nothing. Except when you leave, you have to pay taxes on it.

Diogenes searched the world over and could not find ten honest men— and that was before politics became an art form.

I believe in honesty and integrity. Someone asked me what I would do if I found $1 million in the street. If it belonged to a poor person, I'd give it back.

Today everyone wants instant gratification no matter how long it takes.

I knew I was an unwanted baby when I saw that my bath toys were a toaster and a radio.—*Joan Rivers*

My parents put a live teddy bear in my crib.—*Woody Allen*

To show you how wild my kids are, my eight year old bought a bicycle with the money he saved by not smoking.—*Phyllis Diller*

We had a quicksand box in our backyard. I was an only child, eventually.—*Steven Wright*

. . .

Men never outgrow their love of childhood toys. Many of them never outgrow childhood.

You show me a child who doesn't play with toys, and I'll show you a father who's not done with them yet.

I bought my son a toy that was absolutely guaranteed to be completely unbreakable. He used it to break all his other toys.

Some new toys are so complicated that only a child can operate them.

Kids only want high-technology toys nowadays. My son has an imaginary playmate that requires batteries.

Toys are getting more and more expensive and complicated. I saw one that was $29.95—for the instruction booklet.

There should be a law: anything that costs over $49.95 should not be labeled a plaything.

I saw one toy that was labeled accurately. It said, "recommended for children ages 6 to 12 provided they can get their hands on $46.50."

Why is it that the more expensive a toy is, the more inclined the child is to play with the box it came in?

When I see the words "some assembly required" written on the side of a box, I always feel they should have after them "by a better man than me."

BOOMERANGS

An economist is a guy who'd throw you a boomerang for your birthday.
—*Milton Berle*

. . .

A boomerang is a stick that will always come back to you when you throw it. Maybe it's for kids who like to play fetch, but don't own a dog.

The man who invented the boomerang was hurt in an accident.
Right after he invented it, he forgot to duck.

The question is: If a boomerang always comes back to you after you throw it, why throw it in the first place?

A boomerang always comes back to you no matter where you throw it.
My dad says he wants to invent money like that.

I bought a boomerang that came with a money-back guarantee, but every time I tried to return it, it came back to me.

A boomerang always comes back to you. It's like a yo-yo with no strings attached.

A boomerang always comes back to where it started.
Boy, if I had a memory like that I might be able to pass geography.

Santa Claus gave me a boomerang for Christmas. The next day it went back to the North Pole.

You throw the boomerang as hard as you can, and it winds up right back where it started. I've made golf shots like that.

The boomerang makes a complete circle and comes right back to just about where it started. It's kind of like a cab ride in a strange city.

I once had a car that was part boomerang. No matter where I drove it, it always returned to the dealer's repair shop.

My uncle crossed a boomerang with a homing pigeon. No matter where you threw it, it would return twice.

I knew a guy who once bought a defective boomerang.
He couldn't return it.

 *FOOTBALL*

The Rose Bowl is the only bowl I've seen that I didn't have to clean.
—*Erma Bombeck*

I'm a football fan, but I think there are too many games on over the holidays. At our Thanksgiving dinner, Dolores passed me the turkey and I spiked it. —*Bob Hope*

When I played football, I was known as Crazy Legs until I was 12 years old. That's when I learned to put my pants on with the zipper in front.

Sports are the only entertainment where, no matter how many times you go back, you'll never know the ending.

Football is quite a sport. Every weekend they have to get up early, become hyped up for the game, put their uniforms on—and that's only the fans.

Everybody gets dressed in crazy costumes to go to football games nowadays. I've been to games where the only two creatures in the entire stadium who looked normal were the team mascots.

The fans have a good time. I get the feeling that if football were banned, the fans would still show up every weekend anyway.

Football is getting rough. You have to wear shoulder pads, a face guard, and a helmet—and that's just to sit in the stands.

Football players say the fans are so noisy that they can't even hear themselves think. At most, that would affect maybe one or two players on the team.

They have more fights in the stands each Sunday than Muhammad Ali had in his entire career.

At the Los Angeles Coliseum one Sunday, eight fights broke out in the stands before they realized that the Raiders were playing an away game that weekend.

I know a football fan who always buys two seats—one to sit in and one to use as a weapon when the fight breaks out.

Everybody knows how rowdy the fans get. The vendors go up and down the aisles hollering, "Peanuts, popcorn, bandages . . ."

Football is a violent sport. They do things in this sport that you get penalized for in hockey.

It's getting worse, too. They used to carry the players off the field on a stretcher; now they use a shopping bag.

This one guy was a hard-nosed football player. He was respected, he was feared, he was avoided—and that was in his own huddle.

BASEBALL

Last Christmas, my father gave me a bat. First time I tried to play with it, it flew away.—*Rodney Dangerfield*

A friend gave me seats to the World Series. From where I sat, the game was just a rumor.—*Henny Youngman*

During his playing days, he would kick, scratch, claw—do anything to gain an advantage. It got so rough that his teammates asked that he eat in another dining room.

I like baseball as a sport, because in baseball when you hit a ball into the stands, you just forget about it. In golf, you have to go looking for it.

Baseball is easier than golf. In baseball, you hit the ball and someone else chases it.

I played on a bad baseball team when I was a kid.
The only thing our shortstop caught all year was mononucleosis.

One kid on my team got beaned the other day. The coach said it's the most wood he got on the ball all season.

We got very few hits. If anybody on our team reached first base, he had to stop and ask for directions.

We had such bad hitters. On our team a foul ball was considered a rally.

When I played in choose-up baseball games, they'd tell me to stand out in right field. Then the two teams would go play on another field.

We were losing one game 126 to 0, but we weren't worried. We hadn't had our turn at bat yet.

We only had one victory all season, and that was when the other team didn't show up

Some of our hitters are so bad that they can strike out on two pitches.

—*Milton Berle*

The cost of high baseball salaries is being passed on to the fans. You can't buy a hot dog at the ballpark now unless you can find a co-signer. . . . If you want mustard and relish, you have to mortgage your house.

A player was just signed for over $3 million a season. If I made that much money, I wouldn't steal second. I'd buy it.

Our team lives hockey, it dreams hockey, it eats hockey. Now if it could only play hockey.—*Milton Berle*

Hockey is a game where you take a stick and hit either the puck or anyone who has touched the puck.

Most fans agree that hockey is the fastest game played today. And if any fans don't agree, you hit them across the back of the neck with a hockey stick.

Hockey is a rough-and-tumble game, and tempers do flare occasionally. But wouldn't life be much better today if the world had been designed with a penalty box?

When I was a kid, I thought hockey players who were sent to the penalty box had to sit there until their fathers got home from work. . . . Come to think of it, that's not a bad idea.

There are only three ways to play hockey: rough, rougher, and "I'll help you look for your teeth, if you'll help me look for mine."

Most hockey players aren't big, either. Their bodies are just large enough to carry all the black-and-blue marks they get in a game.

Put it on ice and it's called hockey. Put it in a department store, and it's called the January White Sale.

GOLF

To me, golf is something you did with your hands while you talked. Unless you smoked—then you never had to leave the clubhouse. —*Erma Bombeck*

Golf is the only game, outside of solitaire, where you play alone. What you do with your ball hasn't got anything to do with what the other fellow does with his. It's solitaire, only quieter.—*Will Rogers*

Would you believe that there are 3,000 miniature golf courses in the city of Los Angeles? Half of America is bent over.—*Will Rogers*

Give me my golf clubs, the fresh air, and a beautiful woman as a partner—and you can have the golf clubs and the fresh air.—*George Burns*

You don't have to keep score when you play golf with Jerry Ford. You just look back along the fairway and count the wounded.—*Bob Hope*

Truth is something you leave in the locker room with your street shoes when you play golf.

They have some new equipment in golf now that favors seniors. Like that long putter you put right under your chin. You can putt and take a nap at the same time.

My uncle has a different name for golf—connect the sand traps.
. . . He can play five or six rounds of golf without having the ball touch grass once.

Arnold Palmer makes millions of dollars playing golf, and that's not counting all those dimes he's collected picking up other people's ball markers.

Jerry Ford changed the game of golf. When you're in his foursome, you don't think of the bunkers as hazards. They're more like a form of protection.

You know, people don't mind getting hit by Jerry Ford. They're just glad he didn't take up bowling.

BOXING

I put the P U in pugilism.—*Bob Hope*

That fight was so short that when they raised the winner's arm, I thought it was a deodorant commercial. —*Slappy White*

I went to the boxing matches the other night, and a hockey game broke out.—*Rodney Dangerfield*

I was a pretty good fighter once. I used to be able to take a good punch. The only problem was I'd take it thirty or forty times a round.

I used to run three or four miles right before a fight. But my opponent always caught me and beat me up anyway.

I was noted for my fancy footwork as a boxer. I was disqualified from twelve fights for kicking.

I always had special boxing shorts made when I got into the ring. I needed something to go with the yellow streak down my back.

There was one thing I never got to see in my boxing career
—the end of the first round.

I had to give up boxing for financial reasons. I couldn't afford to buy any more smelling salts.

I was a bad boxer. I got knocked out three times when I was shadow boxing.

It's crazy when you figure boxers get all that money for fighting, and hockey players do it every night for free.

I have a problem with boxing. I don't understand any sport where a guy who makes $11 million is called "the loser."

Boxing is a funny sport. They say, "May the better man win," and then when he does, they attack the referee.

FISHING

All you need to be a fisherman is patience and a worm. —*Herb Shriner*

You never see a fish on the wall with its mouth shut. —*Sally Berger*

Good fishing is just a matter of timing. You have to get there yesterday.
—*Milton Berle*

My husband is one of those fishermen who wear those boots that extend up to the armpits, so that when the water pours in, you are assured of drowning instantly.—*Erma Bombeck*

If you don't do anything the entire day, you're called a bum. If you do it in a boat, you're called a fisherman.

I once knew a one-armed fisherman. He had a terrible time telling you how big the one that got away was.

Every time I try fishing, the fish aren't biting but the mosquitoes are. I think someday I'll go out in a boat and try to go mosquitoing.

I went trout fishing one day with my dumb cousin. As we stood waist-deep in the water, he said, "You know, I wish I was a lot taller because someday I'd like to go deep-sea fishing."

I knew an old fellow who told me once, "In order to catch fish, you have to think like a fish." He's gone now. He drowned one night in his sleep.

Fishing is great recreation. It's just about the most fun you can have with a worm on a string.

I used to enjoy fishing tremendously until one day I happened to look at it from the worm's point of view.

The game warden said, "You've got a worm on your line, you've got the line in the water, and you tell me you're not fishing. What exactly are you doing?" The man said, "I'm carrying out a punishment. This particular worm has been accused of witchcraft."

LIFE'S LITTLE PLEASURES

Favorite Things

Gifts

Compliments

Picnics

The Beach

The Sea

Gardening

Walking

FAVORITE THINGS

All the things I really like to do are either immoral, illegal, or fattening.
—*Alexander Woollcott*

The best things in life are free, and the cheesiest things in life are free
with a paid subscription to Sports Illustrated.—*Johnny Carson*

Many girls like the quiet things in life, like the folding of hundred-dollar
bill.—*Henny Youngman*

. . .

It's easy to catalog my favorite things—anything my spouse and the IRS
hasn't found out about.

One of my favorite things is to have a series of pleasant dreams
. . while I'm at the opera.

Life's greatest pleasures are the simple ones, like seeing the driver who
cut ahead of you on the freeway pulled over by the police 3 miles down
the road.

I have a friend who's such a grouch he only has a few favorite things, and
he doesn't even like them.

I have a friend who's a total pessimist. He says life is full of simple little
pleasures, but the pain is serious.

I enjoy the simple little pleasures of life, but every once in a while I want a big expensive one thrown in there, too.

I have three favorite things: my memories . . . and I forget the other two.

All I need to enjoy life are the three "L's": Love, Laughter, and hitting the Lottery.

GIFTS

I know the perfect gift for the man who has everything—a burglar alarm.—*Milton Berle*

You know what I got for Father's Day? The bills from Mother's Day.
—*Henny Youngman*

I gave my wife a gift certificate for Christmas. She ran out to exchange it for a bigger size.—*Milton Berle*

. . .

I asked my wife what she wanted for our anniversary. She told me to buy something for the house. So I bought a round of drinks.

My spouse said, "I really don't want a gift this year. Let's just do something together." So we had a fight about my not buying a gift.

My husband bought me the perfect gift for my birthday. It's something he's always wanted.

I think the best thing about receiving the perfect gift is taking it back and exchanging it for something better.

My wife said she bought me the perfect gift the other day. She'll give it to me when I'm worthy of it.

They say it's better to give than receive. I've discovered with some gifts, that's true.

For our anniversary I presented my wife with an all-expense-paid trip for two to Tahiti. She's been busy ever since trying to decide who to take with her.

I told my wife that for my birthday I wanted her to give me something I'd never forget. She gave me a string to tie around my finger.

I like to receive the gift of money. You can exchange it for so many nice things.

I told my wife I wanted an antique as a gift. She had my birth certificate framed.

COMPLIMENTS

I have a car that I call Flattery because it gets me nowhere.
—*Henny Youngman*

I've been complimented many times, and that always embarrasses me. I always feel they have not said enough.—*Mark Twain*

I can live for two months on a good compliment.—*Mark Twain*

He paid me a compliment. He said I looked like a breath of spring. Well, he didn't use those words. He said I looked like the end of a hard winter.—*Minnie Pearl*

People tell me, "Gee, you look good." There are three ages of man: youth, middle age, and "Gee, you look good."—*Red Skelton*

I got a wonderful tribute at the airport. They fired 21 shots in the air in my honor. Of course, it would've been nicer if they'd waited for the plane to land.—*Bob Hope*

. . .

This man's an incurable liar, except when he's complimenting me.

I've received ten compliments today—two of them from other people.

Have you noticed? Celebrities all hate critics, but quote them when they give good reviews.

I graciously accept all compliments. One can't argue with the truth.

I told my mother-in-law that in my 25 years of being married to her daughter, she's never said anything nice about me. She asked for a little more time.

If you compliment me, I'll compliment you. There's a good chance one of us might be telling the truth.

Remember, you can catch more flies with a teaspoon of honey than with a barrel of vinegar. Of course, what you're going to do with a bunch of sticky flies is your problem.

I love to listen to compliments. I feel humility should be saved for those who have truly earned it.

Some people say "thank you" after receiving a compliment. I simply nod in agreement.

As far as I'm concerned, you can keep all your compliments to yourself. I much prefer a cash reward.

My spouse always finds some little thing in the morning to compliment me about. Oh, sometimes it takes an hour or more. . . .

I've been collecting compliments all my life. So far I've gotten three.

PICNICS

When the insects take over the world, we hope they will remember with gratitude how we took them along on all our picnics.—*Bill Vaughan*

Watermelon—it's a good fruit. You eat, you drink, you wash your face.
—*Enrico Caruso*

The best form of exercise is picnics. You can use up 2,000 calories trying to keep the ants and flies away from the potato salad.—*Jack E. Leonard*

Insects must have brains. How else would they know that you're going on a picnic?—*Milton Berle*

. . .

Picnics were invented to justify all that potato salad.

Picnics are fun. Anytime there are that many men walking around in short pants, it's got to be a lot of laughs.

The problem with picnics is that they're always held on a holiday —when the ants have the day off, too.

So many ants showed up at our picnic that they won the tug-of-war.

I think history will prove that picnics were invented either by a colony of hungry ants or by a mayonnaise salesman.

Picnics are always held outdoors, because that's where you want to be when the hard-boiled eggs go bad.

Talk about strange bedfellows. How about all the ants who show up at the exterminators' picnic?

Our family is so large that every year I go to the cousins' picnic to meet new friends.

Our family always asks Aunt Matilda to make her tuna surprise for the cousins' picnic. It's the best thing we've found yet to keep the flies away. . . . Or to punish those flies who do show up.

The bad news is that I got poison ivy at our cousins' picnic. The worse news is that I got it from Aunt Matilda's green salad.

We always end our cousins' picnic with a fireworks display —*Aunt Matilda and Uncle Harvey's marital problems.*

THE BEACH

When I go to the beach I don't tan, I stroke.—*Woody Allen*

The girls are wearing less and less on the beach, which is perfect for me because my memory is starting to go.—*Bob Hope*

This girl was so thin, every time she went to the beach, a dog buried her.—*Milton Berle*

The town was so dull that when the tide went out it refused to come back.—*Fred Allen*

I never expected to see the day when girls would get sunburned in the places they do today.—*Will Rogers*

I went to the beach the other day. I held my stomach in so much I threw out my back.—*Milton Berle*

I won't say her bathing suit was skimpy, but I've seen more cotton in the top of an aspirin bottle.—*Henny Youngman*

. . .

I don't look good on the beach. I look like I'm wearing my inner tube internally.

The beach is where you wear practically nothing at all and
it fills with sand.

Bathing suits don't shrink in water. They shrink when they're stored
in the closet during the winter.

Vacation is when you can lie on the beach and get burned
by the sun and also by the hotel where you're booked.

The sales clerk said, "That bathing suit fits you perfectly." I said,
"Sure, that's what you said about the one I bought here last year, too."

I bought a bathing suit that said, "one size fits all" and proved it wrong.

I look so bad in a bathing suit, the lifeguard asked me to go
for a swim the other day—to scare any sharks away.

I had a close call at the beach last week. I swallowed too much
sand from trying to suck in my stomach.

The other day I sat for hours on the beach hoping to watch the sunrise.
Finally, someone was nice enough to tell me I was facing the wrong way.
. . . I got a terrible burn on my back.

Last week I fell asleep on the beach with my mouth open. My tongue got
sunburned.
. . . It took a good two weeks before I could say "Theophilus."

THE SEA

I have a large seashell collection which I keep scattered along the beaches around the world. Maybe you've seen it.—*Steven Wright*

Why does the ocean roar? You'd roar, too, if you had that many crabs on your bottom.—*Redd Foxx*

What about all those detergents which are going out to our rivers and oceans? If this keeps up, it's going to leave a ring around the country. —*John Byner*

Our waters are so dirty, many of our fishes are beaching themselves and asking for asylum.—*Bob Hope*

Our waters are in trouble. The other day a dam gave way, but the lake didn't.—*Milton Berle*

. . .

The sea has a soothing effect. Have you ever seen a nervous clam?

Two-thirds of the Earth's surface is covered with water. That's a lot like my basement when I tried to do my own plumbing.

Some of our fish now have so much mercury in them, they can take their own temperature.

Our oceans are so dirty they have signs at some beaches that read, "Please wipe your feet before leaving the ocean."

You know our waters are getting pretty dirty. Fish have begun washing their food before eating it.

There are so many oil slicks in the oceans now that every time the tide comes in, it slips right out again.

Twice a year all the oceans have to be brought in now for an oil change.

I've heard of tuna packed in oil, but not while they were still swimming around.

When an octopus puts on deodorant, how does he remember where he started?

Fish is supposed to be brain food. How much brain does it take to bite into a plastic worm with a hook in it?

I'm not a fish eater. The only seafood I'll eat is salt-water taffy.
. . . unless it has bones in it.

GARDENING

Did you see the pictures of the moon? They must have the same gardener I have.—*Harry Hershfield*

I like to tease my plants. I water them with ice cubes.—*Steven Wright*

I don't exactly have a green thumb. I once killed a flagpole.
—*Milton Berle*

I don't have the knack for growing houseplants. I bought a hanging fern and the rope died.—*Milton Berle*

I have bad luck with plants. I bought a philodendron and put it in the kitchen. It drank my soup.—*Joan Rivers*

. . .

I have bad luck with plants. I have a chia pet that attacked the mailman.

I'm a terrible gardener. I tried to plant some flowers along my driveway. The asphalt died.

I'm a bad gardener. I have a green thumb that has dry rot.

I can't do anything right with plants. I bought a Venus fly trap. It turned out to be a vegetarian.

I can't raise houseplants at all. The guy at the nursery said I should talk to them. All I can say to them is "Rest in peace."

I'm such a terrible gardener they have a Wanted poster of me hanging at the local nursery.

I paid a fortune for a philodendron. It died before I learned how to spell it.

I'm such a terrible gardener, if anyone comes to my yard and asks, "What kind of plant is that?" I say, "A dead one."

 **WALKING**

Everywhere is within walking distance if you have the time.
—*Steven Wright*

I like long walks, especially when they are taken by people who annoy me.—*Fred Allen*

My grandmother started walking 5 miles a day when she was 60. She's 93 today and we don't know where the hell she is.—*Ellen Degeneres*

Most people agree that walks are good for your health. Where I live in Beverly Hills, nobody walks. I've got one neighbor who has a little car to drive to his big car.—*George Burns*

The true charm of pedestrianism does not lie in the walking, or in the scenery, but in the talking.—*Mark Twain*

. . .

I own a pair of microwave walking shoes. I can now take a leisurely walk in the country in 2 1/2 minutes.

The only thing better than an early-morning walk with someone you love is to have someone you love take an early-morning walk without you and then wake you when she gets home.

Walking is probably the greatest form of exercise there is, unless you're in water. Then swimming is better.

Short walks can be very romantic, especially if they're up the center aisle of a church.

I looked at a good pair of walking shoes the other day. They cost $120. For that kind of money I could take a cab.
. . . Imagine that: $120 for a pair of walking shoes. Centipedes don't realize how lucky they are that they can go barefoot.

Sometimes I dream I'm walking, which is nice. I get my rest and exercise all at the same time.
. . . It's a fair exchange—I usually dream when I'm walking, too.

PEOPLE WE KNOW &LOVE —OR DON'T

Egomaniacs

Bores

Latecomers

Couch Potatoes

Grouches

Cheapskates

Crazies

EGOMANIACS

I talk to myself because I like dealing with a better class of people
—*Jackie Mason*

This guy is such an egotist, the towels in his bathroom are marked "His" and "His."—*Milton Berle*

He is a very religious man. He worships himself. —*Jack E. Leonard*

The last time I saw him, he was walking down Lovers' Lane holding his own hand.—*Fred Allen*

. . .

An egomaniac is a guy who thinks he's always right, and he's wrong.

I hate egotists. They all think they're as good as I am.

I dreamed I was the Ruler of the Entire World last night. When my alarm clock went off, I had it beheaded.

I know a guy who thinks he's God's gift to women. And all the women are hoping the gift is returnable.

If this guy's head were any bigger, his hat size would be the same as his zip code.

This guy's head would swell up so often that he had to wear an expandable hat.

He once said to me, "I'm the greatest thing on Earth." I said, "You've got yourself confused with a circus."

I knew one egomaniac who actually thought that he was humble. He used to say: "Some geniuses are conceited, but I'm not."

One friend of mine used to look in the mirror and think he was handsome. He was either an egomaniac or nearsighted.

He's the kind of egotist who could go through hell with a holier-than-thou attitude.

BORES

Everyone says he has a dull personality. That's not true
—he has no personality at all.—*Morey Amsterdam*

. . .

This guy is so dull! At parties people would mistake him for the cheese dip.

This guy is so boring, the most excitement he's ever had in his life was once when he entered a fingernail-growing contest.
. . . He lost. He said the most he could ever grow was ten.

Talk about dull! This guy has the personality of a soupspoon.
. . . And he gets invited to just about as many parties.

This guy is so dull, he once joined a computer dating service and they matched him with lard.

This guy is not exciting. Getting your toe stuck in the bathtub faucet is more fun than being with him.

This guy is so dull that when he goes to a party, the party goes somewhere else.

Anyone who claims that nothing exists in a vacuum has never seen this guy's personality.

This guy has all the excitement of a wet wick at a fireworks display.

This man is dull. He was once almost attacked by a shark. The shark circled him three times and lost interest.

LATE-COMERS

I have the feeling that there's a correlation between getting up in the morning and getting up in the world.—*Milton Berle*

. . .

I know one guy who arrives late for everything. In fact, our rule of thumb is that if you don't get there before he does, there's no sense going.

This kid I know arrives late for everything. He was three years old at his first birthday party.

This boy has always been late for everything. His twin brother is six months older than he is.

This guy is always late—even for ball games. He thinks the words to the national anthem are ". . . and the home of the brave play ball."

This guy is always late. He threw a New Year's Eve party for all his friends last March 15th.

This guy arrives at parties so late that he has to bring his own cheese dip.

This guy arrives so late at parties that by the time he throws his coat in the bedroom, the host and hostess are already asleep in it.

All through his education, the only time he wasn't late for school was when he was absent.
. . . And he would've been late for that if he could have been there.

If you want this guy to be someplace on time, it's safer to invite someone else.

COUCH POTATOES

Fang can't stand to see trash and garbage lying around the house. He can't stand the competition.—*Phyllis Diller*

I should have suspected my husband was lazy when his mother told me on our wedding day: "I'm not losing a son; I'm gaining a couch."
—*Phyllis Diller*

I can't go to work because I have trouble with my back. I can't get it off the bed.—*Jackie Mason*

There is no radical cure for laziness, but starvation will come the nearest to it.—*Josh Billings*

The laziest man I ever met put popcorn in his pancakes so they would turn over by themselves.—*W. C. Fields*

. . .

I do some work around the house once in a while. The last time I worked up a sweat, my wife didn't wash my work shirt—she framed it.

I'm so lazy I never turn the ball game on until the second inning. I'm afraid I might be a little early and have to stand for the national anthem.

I know a guy who is so lazy, he likes to do absolutely nothing at all. He just closes his eyes and pretends he's a politician.

He spends his entire day half-asleep. He just leaves word for his family not to move him at all unless he's on fire.

His biggest decision is deciding whether he wants salt or pepper on his eggs in the morning. He's too lazy to shake both.

He's too lazy even to wind a self-winding watch. He slips it on his dog's tail and then makes a fuss over him.

The only way he brushes his teeth is barefoot on the cold marble floor. He figures it's less work if he just holds the brush still and lets his teeth chatter.

He taught his dog to fetch, but he's so lazy that he also taught him to throw the stick, too.

GROUCHES

Start every day off with a smile and get it over with.—*W. C. Fields*

There are only a few things in this life that give me pleasure,
and I can't stand them.—*Gene Perret*

. . .

I know a guy who was such a miserable grouch that at his funeral, the
only pallbearers they could get were six guys who had never met him.

I knew one kid who was miserable about everything. At his birthday
party, he didn't blow out the candles—he chased them home.

I knew one woman who had such a terrible frown on her face all the time
that when she put on her make-up, it curdled.

This woman is such a grouch that no one goes near her. The stork left her
baby two blocks away, and she had to go pick it up.

CHEAP SKATES

I took my date to dinner last night. She was so excited, she dropped her
tray.—*Jack Benny*

Fang took the entire family out for coffee and donuts the other night. The kids enjoyed it. It was the first time they'd ever given blood.
—*Phyllis Diller*

Cheap? His hearing aid is on a party line.—*Henny Youngman*

This guy is so cheap he won't even eat in the sun for fear his shadow will ask him for a bite.—*Jack Benny*

. . .

This friend of mine is the cheapest man I've ever known. He still has the first dollar he ever borrowed.

This guy is so cheap that he not only has the first dollar he ever made, but also the arm of the man who handed it to him.

This guy is so cheap that he always leaves a 20-percent tip
—20 percent of what anyone else would leave.

My wife says I'm so cheap I only open my wallet for two reasons
—to put money in and to let the guard out on his day off.

It's not that I'm cheap. I just hate to give money away after I've memorized the serial numbers.

I had a friend who was so cheap that he borrowed a suit to be buried in.

This guy owes so much money to so many people, his answering machine just says, "Hi, your check is in the mail."

He's so cheap he'd like to put a few bucks into the stock market, but all his money is sewn into his mattress.

This guy is so cheap he won't buy deodorant. He buys a soap that odor-proofs the body for 12 hours, and keeps turning the clock back.

CRAZIES

I just read that one out of every four people is mentally unbalanced. Try it; think of three of your best friends. . . . If they seem all right to you—you're the one.—*Slappy White*

There is a thin line between genius and insanity. I have erased that line.
—*Oscar Levant*

· · ·

They asked my Uncle Wally if anybody in his family suffers from insanity. He said, "No, they all seem to be enjoying it."

People considered my Uncle Mort crazy because he always wore one red sock and one blue one—instead of trousers and a suit coat.

We had one guy in our neighborhood who thought he was a rooster. It was sad. The day after he died, everyone overslept.

I had a friend who was a paranoid schizophrenic. He always thought he was following himself.

One friend of mine always thought he was too short to amount to anything. I convinced him that was crazy. When he left my house that night, a cat ate him.

I had an aunt who thought she was the Queen of England. I would have told her how insane that was, but I didn't want to blow my chance at knighthood.

I had one aunt who thought she was the Goodyear blimp. Sure, it sounds crazy to you, but she got to see a lot of football games for free.

LOOKS ARE EVERYTHING

Fashion

The Worst Dressed

Appearance

Beauty

Big Eaters

Skinnies

Bodybuilders

Baldies

Barbershop Talk

Broken Combs

FASHION

Heaven knows, I try to bend the dictates of fashion, but I'm a loser. When I grew my own bustle, they went out of style.—*Erma Bombeck*

Clothes make the man. Naked people have little or no influence in society.—*Mark Twain*

It's hard to buy a negligee in my size. I wear a Junior Mister.
—*Phyllis Diller*

I base most of my fashion taste on what doesn't itch.—*Gilda Radner*

. . .

This girl's dress was tighter than my skin. I can sit down in my skin.

I don't know where the girls get some of those bikinis. No one knows where they buy them; they're not big enough to hold a label.

Dress shoes nowadays are ones that don't have Reebok written across them.

There are three categories of clothes to wear to parties now
—formal, semiformal, and sweat.

I went to a cocktail party the other night, and I felt terribly overdressed. I was the only one wearing a velour warm-up suit.

He always had a sharp crease in his trousers
—even when he wasn't wearing any.

He wore a shirt and tie everywhere—even into the shower.

He not only had his shoes shined each morning, but his socks
and feet, too.

At his own funeral he made the undertaker feel underdressed.

He wore a shirt, tie, and business suit no matter where he went
or what he did. It made swimming laps at the YMCA a little messy.

He was such a meticulous dresser. If you saw a thread hanging
from his clothing, chances are it was supposed to be there.

He was always careful about his clothing. As an infant, he used to
change his own diapers.

THE WORST DRESSED

Last Saturday my husband wore sneakers, sweat socks, khakis with paint
all over them, and a white shirt open at the collar with the undershirt
showing. I was too embarrassed to introduce him to the bride.
—*Phyllis Diller*

Once I opened a closet and a moth had eaten my sports jacket. He was
lying on the floor nauseous.—*Woody Allen*

I wasn't dressed properly because you don't wear argyles with dark blue. I had on dark blue socks and an argyle suit.—*Woody Allen*

You look like a million bucks—all wrinkled and green.
—*Henny Youngman*

. . .

I can be a neat dresser. When we go formal, I insist that the tuxedo trousers just touch the top of my sandals.

I dress so badly that my wife doesn't want people to know I'm her husband. When I open the door for her, she tips me.

One of my friends is even worse. His pants are so baggy in the seat and so droopy in the knees that from the side he looks like the Mark of Zorro.

His sweater has every color in the rainbow and even a few colors that rainbows won't wear in public.

He took some of his old sweaters and threw them in the Goodwill bin. The bin threw them back out.

For such a well-to-do man, he dresses terribly. He never lets success go to his clothing.

Nothing he wears ever matches. We think he buys all his clothes at Hart, Schaffner, Barnum & Bailey.

APPEARANCE

My nose was so big when I was a kid that I thought it was a third arm.
—*David Brenner*

"Hey, where are my glasses?""On your nose.""Be more specific."
—*Jimmy Durante*

You won't believe this—but I was an ugly baby. I was so ugly my mother used to diaper my face.—*Jackie Mason*

I'm the only woman who can walk in Central Park at night and reduce the crime rate.—*Phyllis Diller*

When I go to the beach, even the tide won't come in.—*Phyllis Diller*

She had the biggest overbite in Brooklyn. She used to eat a piece of toast and finish the outer edges first.—*Woody Allen*

. . .

I knew a girl who was so heavy that when her husband carried her over the threshold, he had to make two trips.

Talk about heavy. She's the only woman I know who looks the same sitting down as she does standing up.

Her husband is as heavy as she is. They had to be married in adjoining churches.

My friend is so heavy that when she visits Rhode Island, parts of her hang over into Connecticut.

This woman is very popular at church picnics. She can provide the entire congregation with shade.

This woman was so heavy that last month she lost four girdles—while she was wearing them.

This woman was so overweight that when she took her girdle off, her feet disappeared.

He was big even as a child. It took them until he was six years old to figure out he wasn't twins.

He's so big he has to have all his clothes custom-made. Not by a tailor— by a contractor.

His nose doesn't look like a nose. It looks like something you'd carry spare parts in.

I look so awful in the morning, I had the mirror put on the inside of the medicine chest.

 **BEAUTY**

My wife went to the beauty parlor and got a mud pack. For two days she looked nice. Then the mud fell off.—*Henny Youngman*

I remember how excited I got one day when I discovered a cosmetic stick that could erase away wrinkles. I erased my entire face.—*Erma Bombeck*

I spent seven hours in a beauty shop, and that was for the estimate.
—*Phyllis Diller*

Most people get an appointment at a beauty parlor—I was committed.
—*Phyllis Diller*

. . .

Beauty is only skin deep, which is all right—that's as far as most of us can see anyway.

Some say that beauty is only skin deep, but ugly goes all the way to the bone.

True beauty can be a curse. Unfortunately, I'm only a mild invective.

I knew a girl who went to beauty college and flunked cosmetics. They let her take a make-up exam.

Some women take over an hour to put on their natural beauty.

Men are going to beauty parlors now, too. It's the macho thing to do. All over the country I can just hear guys saying, "I'm gonna run down to the corner and get a couple of beers and a body wax."

BIG EATERS

Fang says he eats a lot to settle his nerves. I said, "Have you seen where they're settling?"—*Phyllis Diller*

My favorite meal is breakfast, lunch, dinner, and in-between.
—*Totie Fields*

My wife is so fat that every time she gets into a cab, the driver rushes her to the hospital.—*Dave Barry*

I won't tell you how much I weigh, but don't get in an elevator with me—unless you're going down.—*Jack E. Leonard*

She's so fat, she's got more chins than the Chinese telephone directory.
—*Joan Rivers*

. . .

This guy eats all the time. He had two teeth pulled last week. They weren't decayed, just exhausted.

This guy has such an appetite! He can eat an entire cake by himself—while it's baking.

They say this guy eats like a bird. That means when he gets hungry enough, he'll swoop down and scoop up an entire baby goat.

This guy reminds you of a chipmunk—except instead of storing food up for the winter, he stores food up for lunch.

This guy has the appetite of a shark that is going on Weight Watchers tomorrow.

What an appetite! This guy will eat anything that's standing still. He'll eat anything that's moving, too; only it takes him longer.

 SKINNIES

If it weren't for my Adam's apple, I'd have no shape at all.
—Phyllis Diller

There was a time when I had a 23-inch waist. I was 10 years old—my measurements were 23–23–23.—*Erma Bombeck*

I ate more than you for breakfast.—*Jackie Gleason*

This man was so skinny, he was a waste of skin.—*Fred Allen*

This girl was so skinny, she once got a tattoo and it had to be continued on a friend.

My wife is so skinny that when she wears a fur coat, she looks like a pipe cleaner.

I'll give you an idea of how skinny this girl is. She can put her slacks on over her head.

My girl is so skinny that when she wears a ring, it can easily slip off her finger—in either direction.

This girl is so thin, she wore a strapless gown once, and I don't know what held it up—or why!

This girl is so skinny that she's the only one in her family with a fur coat. She made it herself—skinned a caterpillar.

This girl is so skinny that she once wore a green dress and every one wanted to know if she was poisonous.

My girl is so skinny that for a masquerade party she put on a fur hat and fuzzy slippers and went as a Q-tip.

BODY BUILDERS

This kid has muscles everywhere. He can bench-press 250 pounds—with his eyebrows.—*Bob Hope*

This guy has muscles in places where I don't even have places.
—*Bob Hope*

. . .

This is one big guy. He has a ship tattooed on his chest—actual size.

School kids nowadays are taking steroids to grow muscles. They enter their freshman year as a nerd and graduate as a Neanderthal.

Is that guy big and strong or what? I've seen John Deere tractors that weren't built that well.

Look at the size of this guy! I've heard a lot of sonic booms, but this is the first time I've ever met one.

Look at the size of this boy, and this is just the basic model. All of his real muscles he left packed in his gym bag.

My gym teacher said I could be a real muscleman if I wanted to be. He says I have the head for it.

I tried to go to a gym to build up my physique, but it was too much work. So I just gave my instructor the money and asked him to walk me home at night.

BALDIES

Barbers don't charge him for cutting his hair. They charge him for searching for it.—*Henny Youngman*

There's one good thing about being bald. It's neat.—*Milton Berle*

I'm not exactly bald—I simply have an exceptionally large part.
—*Jack E. Leonard*

Because of my father, I'm going bald. When I was a kid, my father got mad and he used to hit me in the head and he loosened my hair. Now it's falling out.—*Sid Caesar*

His hair is getting thinner—but who wants fat hair.—*Milton Berle*

What did the bald man say when he got a comb for his birthday? "Thanks very much. I'll never part with it."—*Larry Wilde*

He really isn't bald-headed—he just has a tall face.—*Milton Berle*

The best thing about being bald is when her folks come home, all you have to do is straighten your tie.—*Milton Berle*

• • •

There's only one real cure for baldness—hair.

There's a good reason why bald people don't get dandruff—they have no place to keep it.

My uncle bought a cheap toupee made out of dog hair, but every time he passes a fire hydrant, one end of it lifts up.

My Uncle Wally said he never saw a bald dog, so he injected himself with cocker spaniel hormones. Now he's got a nice head of wavy hair, but his ears keep flopping in his food.
. . . He's also got fleas.
. . . And Aunt Mabel won't let him up on the couch.

Some people don't mind being bald and others do. Men generally handle it better than women.

My Uncle Wally tried to invent a potion that would grow hair on a billiard ball, but he made a mistake. Now his head is covered with green felt.
. . . And instead of dandruff, he has chalk dust.

My Uncle Ralph always thought he had wavy hair until he went bald. It was his head that was wavy.

My doctor said he would cure my baldness but it would cost me $3,000. I said, "What do I get if it doesn't work?" He said, "A free comb."

My Uncle Wally is so bald he has to buy hats with nonskid sweatbands.

My Uncle Phil says he's not bald. He's just taller than his hair.

My Uncle Phil is totally bald. My Aunt Myrtle calls him the human thumb.

My Uncle Phil tried to invent a lotion that would grow hair on a billiard ball. It worked—partly. He's still bald, but he likes to sleep at night on the pool table.

My Uncle Ralph sprained his neck trying to cure his baldness. He grew a beard and tried to put his head on upside down.

My Uncle Phil is so bald that at night Aunt Myrtle uses his head to read by.

I'm not really bald. My hair is just hibernating.

My uncle says he has a "receding hairline." It has receded all the way back to his neck.

The bad news is some bald people still have dandruff. The good news is they have a lot more room for it.

I asked my doctor, "What's the best thing for baldness?" He said, "A sense of humor."

BARBERSHOP TALK

The barber held up a mirror to see if I liked my new haircut. I said, "Make it a little longer."—*Jackie Kahane*

That's a great barbershop. I used to go there for a shave and an overcoat.—*Milton Berle*

160

When one barber shaves another, who does the talking?—*Milton Berle*

. . .

My buddy puts so much grease in his hair, when he sits in the chair the barber says, "Do you want a haircut or an oil change?"

My barber said, "Why don't you try something different for a change? " I said, "Okay, this time give me a good haircut."

I always laugh at my barber's jokes. After all, he does have a razor in his hand.

My barber has a very sharp wit. I just wish he had scissors to match.

I asked my barber why he ties that cloth around my neck so tight. He said, "In case I cut you, it doubles as a tourniquet."

My barber said he hates the sight of blood, so he puts a blindfold on when he shaves me.

I told my barber to be careful while he was working on me; I didn't want him to cut my ear off. He said, "Don't worry. I have a drawer full of spares."

My barber said, "I've been in business 35 years and have never lost an ear." I said, "That's nice, but how about your customers?"

BROKEN COMBS

I said to my hairdresser, "What would look good on me? He said, "A Los Angeles Rams football helmet."—*Phyllis Diller*

I always wanted to turn to my hairdresser and say, "If I wanted hair the consistency and style of a steel helmet, I could have been a Viking."
—*Erma Bombeck*

I comb my hair with an electric toothbrush.—*Phyllis Diller*

. . .

She wore so much hair spray that when you ran your fingers through her hair, you had to count them afterwards.

She wore so much hair spray that once she bumped her head and fractured three curls.

Her ponytail was too tight. Every time she blinked her mouth popped open.

Everyone told her that her ponytail was too tight. One's ears should not touch in the back of one's head.

OPPOSITES ATTRACT

Short & Tall

Superiority & Inferiority

Lying & Truth

Old & Young

Friends & Enemies

Rich & Poor

Love & Hate

SHORT & TALL

I started in show business when I was fourteen and only the size of a kid of ten. By twenty, though, I'd shot up to the size of a kid of eleven.
—*Morey Amsterdam*

I feel sorry for short people, you know. When it rains, they're the last to know.—*Rodney Dangerfield*

He's the only man I know that can milk a cow standing up.—*Fred Allen*

I'm not fat at all. . . . I'm just short for my weight. I should be 9'7".
—*Totie Fields*

. . .

He was so tiny that he could wear a short-sleeve shirt with French cuffs.

He was so short he had to stand on a chair to change his mind.

He was so short he could get lost in shag carpeting.

I won't say he was short, but he could look for his shoes under the bed without bending over.

He was so short he had to grow another 6 inches before his friends would call him Shorty.

It was annoying how he was always complaining about being so short. So one day I just stepped on him.

He was so tall that when he fell down, he had to make two trips.

He was so tall that when he bent over to tie his shoelaces, his feet would have to meet him halfway.

He was so tall he had a schooner tattooed on his chest . . . actual size.

He was very tall and thin. He looked like a flagpole with hair.

SUPERIORITY & INFERIORITY

I often quote myself. It adds spice to my conversation.
—*George Bernard Shaw*

Every time I leave the house, my wife tells me to call her in case something goes right.—*Rodney Dangerfield*

He has a terrible inferiority complex and he's right.—*Milton Berle*

I get no respect. I get mail that begins, "You may already be a loser."
—*Rodney Dangerfield*

My mother always taught me to be kind to my inferiors, but she never told me what to do when I was in a room where I didn't have any.
—*Bob Hope*

Dial-a-Prayer hung up on me.—*Jackie Vernon*

"The meek shall inherit the earth." They won't have the nerve to refuse it.—*Jackie Vernon*

Do you ever feel like the whole world's a tuxedo and you're a pair of brown shoes?—*George Gobel*

My only regret in life is that I'm not someone else.—*Woody Allen*

. . .

I know a guy who has such an ego that when he prays he says, "Dear God, do you need anything?"

This guy thinks he's just a little better than everybody else. When he spells his name, he capitalizes the first two letters.

This gentleman has such a big head that when he wears a ten-gallon hat, it's one gallon too small.

His head is so big that his ears are in separate zip codes.

This guy admits he has no humility, but if he did have it, it would be better than everybody else's.

No matter what this guy does, he thinks that no one can hold a candle to him, although a lot of people would like to.

Here's a guy with a giant ego. When he went to see Mt. Rushmore his first words were, "Hey guys, move over."

This guy's ego is so big that when he gets on a plane, it won't fit in the overhead compartment.

This guy casts two shadows—one for him and one for his ego.

His ego is so big that it comes with its own carrying case.
. . . If it weren't on wheels, he couldn't haul it around.

This guy once wrote a book called The Ten Greatest People in History and My Views on the Other Nine.

I'd like to have an inferiority complex, but I don't think I'm good enough.

I thought I had an inferiority complex, but it turned out to be just good judgment.

I know a lot of people with inferiority complexes, but theirs are all better than mine.

There's only one thing worse than feeling inferior, and that's being able to prove it.

I told the doctor I sometimes feel so inferior that I don't think anyone notices me at all. He said, "Next."

Because I feel inferior I try harder. Because I am inferior it doesn't do any good.

I have two basic problems. I think everyone else is better than me and so do they.

My doctor convinced me that my inferiority complex was all in my mind, which he also convinced me is not as good as everybody else's.

The doctor told me he's seen inferiority complexes much worse than mine. Even my inferiority complex is inferior.

I had an inferiority complex even as a kid. I had an imaginary playmate who was ashamed to hang around with me.

I had an inferiority complex very early. At birth, when the doctor slapped my bottom I didn't cry. I felt I deserved it.

LYING & TRUTH

There are three kinds of lies—lies, damned lies, and statistics.
—*Mark Twain*

There's one way to find out if a man is honest: ask him; if he says yes, you know he's crooked.—*Mark Twain*

If one tells the truth, one is sure, sooner or later, to be found out.
—*Oscar Wilde*

No man has a good enough memory to be a successful liar.
—*Abraham Lincoln*

George Washington said to his father: "If I never tell a lie, how can I get to be president?"—*Red Buttons*

One of the most striking differences between a cat and a lie is that a cat has only nine lives.—*Mark Twain*

My brother-in-law tells people he's a diamond cutter. He mows the lawn—at Yankee Stadium.—*Henny Youngman*

My wife never lies about her age. She just tells people she's as old as I am, then she lies about my age.—*Milton Berle*

I told my wife the truth. I told her I was seeing a psychiatrist. Then she told me the truth: that she was seeing a psychiatrist, two plumbers, and a bartender.
—*Rodney Dangerfield*

Why is it when you tell a series of truths and a series of lies, people believe the lies?

The truth will never hurt you . . . unless you're talking to a new parent with a terribly unattractive child.

Anybody who says "Truth is stranger than fiction" has never read Stephen King.

When I tell a lie my palms get sweaty. When I tell the truth, the people I'm talking about get sweaty.

Pinocchio's nose got bigger every time he told an untruth. It kept him out of politics.

My mother always said "Tell the truth and shame the devil." I told the truth once and shamed my father.

My wife has been lying about her age for 15 years now. It started when she was 5 years younger.

Is wearing a toupee a lie? Or is it just a very funny- looking near-truth?

Your lips may lie, but your eyes will always tell the truth. This may give you a little insight into why Tonto never quite trusted the Lone Ranger.

OLD & YOUNG

My husband was old. Ooooold. Older than his birthday.—*Moms Mabley*

Middle age is when work is a lot less fun, and fun is a lot more work.
—*Milton Berle*

Life would be infinitely happier if we could only be born at the age of 80
and gradually approach 18.—*Mark Twain*

An old man can't do nothin' for me except bring me a message from a
young man.—*Moms Mabley*

He is so old that his birth certificate is on a rock.—*Jack Benny*

You're getting older when it takes you more time to recover than it did to
tire you out.—*Milton Berle*

Anyone can get old. All you have to do is live long enough.
—*Groucho Marx*

Every morning when I get up, I read the obituary page. If my name's not
there, I shave.—*George Burns*

There are certain signs when you're old. I walked past the cemetery the
other day and two guys ran after me with shovels.—*Rodney Dangerfield*

He's so old, his blood type is discontinued.—*Bill Dana*

I'll tell you how to keep looking young: hang around with older people.
—*Bob Hope*

He's so old that when he asks for a 3-minute egg, they ask for the money up front.—*Milton Berle*

My husband said when he was young, he used to live in the country.
I said, "When you were young, everybody lived in the country."
—*Moms Mabley*

You know you're old when everybody goes to your birthday party and stands around the cake just to get warm. —*George Burns*

The secret of staying young is to live honestly, eat slowly, and lie about your age.—*Lucille Ball*

I have everything now I had 20 years ago—except now it's all lower..
—*Gypsy Rose Lee*

Life begins at forty, but so does arthritis and the habit of telling the same story three times to the same person.—*Sam Levenson*

Remember that as a teenager you are at the last stage in your life when you will be happy to hear that the phone is for you.—*Fran Lebowitz*

When you are eight years old, nothing is your business.—*Lenny Bruce*

It's a good idea to have children while your parents are still young enough to take care of them.—*Rita Rudner*

I'll never forget my youth. I was the teacher's pet. She couldn't afford a dog.—*Rodney Dangerfield*

When I was young I had the cutest little button nose, but they couldn't feed me. It was buttoned to my lower lip.—*Henny Youngman*

. . .

At my age, I refuse to wear a beeper. I don't want anything else on my body that might fall off.

Age gets to all of us sooner or later. It walks right up to you and says, "Do you know where I can find Dick Clark?"

He's so old that when he plays golf, he doesn't have to yell "Fore." His creaking bones warn the foursome ahead of him.

Youth can be a wonderful thing if you're young enough to enjoy it.

We knew they were too young to get married when they insisted on going to summer camp for their honeymoon.

Childish behavior: that's anyone who is doing what we only wish we could still do.

Middle-aged: that's what old people insist on calling themselves.

She couldn't wait to be old enough to get a face-lift so that she could look younger.

He wore a toupee that made him look about ten years sillier.

Young people keep wanting to look older, and old people keep wanting to look younger. Middle-aged people just keep looking for their reading glasses.

Old people just seem wiser because all they have to fool are the young people.

Middle age is a time of life when the most fun you have is talking about the most fun you used to have.

They call it middle age because it's the age at which your middle starts taking over.

FRIENDS & ENEMIES

He has no friends. He brought a parrot home and it told him to get out.
—*Milton Berle*

I don't know what I'd do without you guys, but I'd rather.—*Frank Fay*

He hasn't an enemy in the world . . . but all his friends hate him.
—*Jack E. Leonard*

She's so fat, she's my two best friends.—Joan Rivers

Always forgive your enemies. . . . Nothing annoys them so much.
—*Oscar Wilde*

He's the kind of man who picks his friends—to pieces.—*Mae West*

The holy passion of friendship is so sweet and steady and loyal and enduring a nature that it will last through a whole lifetime . . . if not asked to lend money.—*Mark Twain*

I like him. I have no taste, but I like him.—*Morey Amsterdam*

Harpo: She's her own worst enemy.Groucho: Not while I'm alive she's not.—*Marx Brothers*

My best friend ran away with my wife, and let me tell you, I miss him. —*Henny Youngman*

Every time I look at you, I get a fierce desire to be lonesome. —*Oscar Levant*

. . .

I'm the kind of guy who will always be a friend to people in need. That's because people who are doing all right won't hang around with me.

I have a friend who is loyal, dependable, courageous, and strong. If he were only a St. Bernard, he'd be perfect.

I know a guy who will be my friend for life or until I pay him back the money I owe him, which is the same thing.

My best friend and I get along like brothers—Cain and Abel.

I have some friends who are just like money in the bank. You can only get to them during business hours.

I never turn my back on my friends. I don't trust them that much.

A friend is a guy who will lend you his last buck. An enemy is a guy who already did and now wants it back.

Think about it: If we didn't have enemies, how would we know who our friends are?

An enemy is sometimes nothing more than a friend who got wise to you.

You show me a person who tells you to forgive your enemy, and I'll show you a person who will make a lousy divorce lawyer.

Money is better than poverty, if only for financial reasons.—*Woody Allen*

My neighborhood was so poor that the only ailment anyone could afford was a fever. You starved that.—*George Burns*

My family was so poor we couldn't give my sister a sweet sixteen party until she was twenty-eight.—*Joey Bishop*

When I was a kid, I was so poor I had to wear my brother's hand-me-downs—at the same time he was wearing them.—*Redd Foxx*

I've been rich and I've been poor. Rich is better.—*Sophie Tucker*

Eleven kids in our family. We were so poor we had to wear each other's clothes. It wasn't funny. I had ten sisters.—*Henny Youngman*

I came from a very poor family. They couldn't afford to have children; so our neighbor had me.—*Henny Youngman*

We were so poor, at school I took algebra, history, and overcoats.
—*Jackie Vernon*

Those people were so rich they had a Persian rug made out of real Persians.—*Henny Youngman*

Rich? He takes cabs to drive-in movies.—*Henny Youngman*

Few of us can stand prosperity—another man's, I mean.—*Mark Twain*

. . .

I was very poor when I was a kid. My parents were wealthy, but I was poor.

We were so poor when I was kid that all we had to wear were hand-me-downs, which was tough on me since I was an only child.

I never experienced poverty as a kid. My family couldn't afford it.

They say you can't take it with you. I never got to fool around with it much while I was here.

We never had much, but what we had wasn't ours.

You come into this life with nothing, and you leave with nothing. It's a lot like asking a relative for a loan.

When you get right down to it, rich people are just poor people with money.

I gave my kids all the things I never had as a child . . . and they laughed at them.

I have a friend who's a very rich undertaker. He drives a sports hearse.

It's true that money can't buy happiness, but poverty can't even buy groceries.

I call my weekly salary my take-home pay because it's the only place I can afford to go with it.

I've always wanted to be filthy rich. So far, I've only gotten the first part.

It seems funny that all the people who hate the rich are the same ones who buy lottery tickets.

He might be considered a rich kid. His parents were so prominent they came from both sides of the tracks.

Beverly Hills is a very exclusive community. Costume jewelry here is considered a misdemeanor.
. . . In their telephone books, names aren't listed alphabetically. They're listed by net worth.

These kids were so rich their dad bought them a chauffeur-driven bicycle.

I'll give you an idea of how rich they are. If he ever tried to bury his money in the backyard, the East Coast would have a Grand Canyon, too.

He has the only wallet in the world that, in a pinch, can double as a wheelbarrow.

Rich people go to prisons that are so plush the guards double as caddies. . . . They had a riot at one of those plush prisons a few years ago. Some innocent people were trying to break in.

He's so rich he owns everything in town. If you put a quarter in a pay phone, his voice says, "Thank you."

LOVE & HATE

If opposites attracted, the North Pole and the South Pole would be married and living happily at the Equator.—*Gene Perret*

Love: Everyone says looks don't matter. Age doesn't matter. Money doesn't matter, but I've never met a girl yet who has fallen in love with an old, ugly man who's broke.—*Rodney Dangerfield*

Love conquers all things except poverty and a toothache.—*Mae West*

Love is staying awake all night with a sick child—or a healthy adult.
—*David Frost*

Love is like hash. You have to have confidence in it to enjoy it.
—*Bob Hope*

There's so much romance in Paris, the storks have to wear beepers.
—*Bob Hope*

Everybody hates this guy. If he had a one-man show on Broadway he'd quit because he couldn't get along with the rest of the cast.—*Bob Hope*

I'M IN PRETTY GOOD SHAPE FOR THE SHAPE I'M IN

Health

Hospitals

Doctors,

Dentists & Shrinks

Aches & Pains

Forgetful

Diets

Vegetables

Exercise

Smoking

# *HEALTH*

It's no longer a question of staying healthy. It's a question of finding a sickness that you like.—*Jackie Mason*

"Quit worrying about your health.—It'll go away."—*Robert Orben*

Health nuts are going to feel stupid someday, lying in hospitals dying of nothing.—*Redd Fox*

I personally stay away from health foods. At my age, I need all the preservatives I can get.—*George Burns*

The only way to keep your health is to eat what you don't want, drink what you don't like, and do what you'd rather not.—*Mark Twain*

There's a lot of people in this world who spend so much time watching their health that they haven't the time to enjoy it.—*Josh Billings*

· · ·

I've never been sick a day in my life. Nights I get a little nauseous, but days never.

An apple a day keeps the doctor away; an onion a day keeps everyone away.

It's better to be healthy than wise. If you're sick, it costs you money, but you can be stupid for free.

If you've got your health, you've got everything. And if you don't have your health, sooner or later your doctor has everything.

We are so health-conscious today. But what good is health? It can't buy money.

A friend of mine went to a new health club and lost four pounds immediately. And that was only his first payment.

My uncle ate nothing but oat bran every day of his life, and he lived a healthy, happy life up until the day he fell in love and tried to marry the horse that won the Kentucky Derby.

My grandfather always used to ask me, "What's more important, your money or your health?" I'd say, "My health." He'd say, "Great, can you lend me 20 bucks?"

HOSPITALS

GEORGE: GRACIE, did the nurse ever happen to drop you on your head when you were a baby?
GRACIE: Oh, no, we couldn't afford a nurse, my mother had to do it.
—*George Burns and Gracie Allen*

When you get your hospital bill, you understand why surgeons wear masks in the operating room.—*Sam Levenson*

Hospitals are weird. They put you in a private room and then give you a public gown.—*Milton Berle*

After two days in the hospital, I took a turn for the nurse.—*W. C. Fields*

I had a very tough nurse in the hospital. She had a black belt in nursing.

A hospital is an institution that is dedicated to the cure of disease—
and modesty.
. . . I can't figure out which covers less—the hospital gown or my
insurance company.

Most hospitals have two accident wards. One of them is the kitchen.

But look on the bright side: The food they serve makes the medicine
taste good.

Hospitals now even have outpatient surgery. You come in and have your
surgery and go home the same day. They're finding out you get cured
faster when you don't have to eat hospital food.

DOCTORS, DENTISTS & SHRINKS

Never go to a doctor whose office plants have died.—*Erma Bombeck*

I'm getting fed up with my doctor. He told me I should keep smoking if I
wanted to stop chewing gum.—*Rodney Dangerfield*

My wife wanted a face-lift. The doctors couldn't do that, but for $80 they
lowered her body.—*Henny Youngman*

One time I went to the doctor and told him I had a ringing in my ear. He
said, "Don't answer it."—*Rodney Dangerfield*

My doctor is wonderful. Once, in 1955, when I couldn't afford an operation, he touched up the X rays.—*Joey Bishop*

I went to a psychoanalyst for years—and it helped—now I get rejected from a much better class of girls.—*Woody Allen*

Psychiatry is when you spend $50 an hour to squeal on yourself.
—*Harry Hershfield*

I quit therapy because my analyst was trying to help me behind my back.—*Richard Lewis*

I'm getting fed up with my psychiatrist. I told him I had suicidal tendencies. From now on I have to pay in advance.—*Rodney Dangerfield*

My dentist just put in a tooth to match my other teeth. It has three cavities.—*Milton Berle*

The doctor who performed my surgery is at this banquet tonight. I happened to glance over at him during the meal and his wife was cutting his meat for him.

The doctor told me my operation was fairly routine and not at all complicated. I told him to remember that when he makes out the bill.

My doctor is very conservative. If he doesn't need the money, he doesn't operate.

My doctor told me this operation was absolutely necessary. I said, "For what?" He said, "To send my kids through college."

My doctor gave me a needle that was the biggest thing I ever saw in my life. Well, it was the biggest thing I ever saw until I got his bill for it.

My family doctor is just like my family dog. Neither one of them will come when you call.

My doctor's very good. He guarantees you'll live to be as old as the magazines in his waiting room.

I could never figure out why my dentist had travel magazines in his waiting room. Then one day he hit a nerve, and I jumped all the way to Cleveland.

My dentist went to dental school in Texas. He keeps drilling until he strikes oil.

Dentists are different from anybody else. For one thing, they're the only people who will invite you to spit in their sink.

My psychiatrist found out that I have two personalities—so he charged me twice as much. I paid him half and said, "Get the rest from the other guy."

I told the psychiatrist I thought everybody hated me because I was so good-looking. He said, "You don't need a psychiatrist; you need a mirror."

I told the psychiatrist I keep hearing strange voices in my ear. He said,

"Where do you want to hear them?"

I went to a psychiatrist for years to get my head on straight. After all that time and money, I found out it was only my tie that was on crooked.

I tried to make an appointment with my shrink, but he couldn't take me. He was having a visit with his shrink.

I asked my shrink to show me one positive result from all my visits. He showed me his new Porsche.

ACHES & PAINS

I told my doctor, "It hurts when I do this." He said, "Don't do that."
—*Henny Youngman*

I'm not into working out. My philosophy: no pain, no pain.—*Carol Leifer*

I went up to visit the doctor with my sore foot. He said, "I'll have you walking in an hour." He did. He stole my car.—*Henny Youngman*

When I was young, if any of us kids got sick, my mother would bring out the chicken soup. Of course, that didn't work for broken bones. For broken bones she gave boiled beef.—*George Burns*

My doctor said, "Have you ever had this pain before?" I said, "Yes." He said, "You've got it again."—*Henny Youngman*

I asked my doctor what to do for a sprained ankle. He said, "Limp."
—*Milton Berle*

. . .

I have so many aches and pains that I list liniment as one of my hobbies.

The only parts of my body that don't hurt are parts that don't work anymore.

When I get out of bed in the morning, the only thing on me that doesn't hurt is my pajamas.

I have so many aches and pains! If it weren't for Ace bandages, I'd have no wardrobe at all.

I had a muscle that twitched all day yesterday. It's the most exercise I've had in years.

The other day my foot fell asleep. The embarrassing part was that it snored.

I had tennis elbow for so long that I finally had to take up the game.

I had some strange ailment where I broke out in little dots all over my body. I asked my doctor what I should do. He said, "Don't wear plaid."

I told my doctor I couldn't lift my hands above my head. He told me to stay away from muggers.

I told my doctor I wanted to do some traveling, but I had all these aches and pains. He taught me how to say "Ow!" in six different languages.

My mommy used to use kisses to make my hurts go away. My doctor says he'll stick with aspirin.

POOR EYESIGHT

I have such poor vision, I could date anyone.—*Garry Shandling*

I'm so nearsighted, I can't even see my contact lenses.
—*Henny Youngman*

The only reason I wear glasses is for little things—like driving my car—
or finding it.—*Woody Allen*

How are your eyes, Mama? You still see spots in front of them? Put on
your glasses. How is it now? You see the spots much clearer.
—*George Jessel*

This woman is so cross-eyed, she can go to a tennis match and never
move her head.—*Phyllis Diller*

I have poor eyesight. When I take an eye test, the doctor points to the letters and he calls them out and says, "True or false?"—*Woody Allen*

. . .

Nature's wonderful. The older-looking you get, the harder it is to see
yourself in the mirror.

You know you've reached middle age when everything in the contract is
in small print.

What scares me is that all those people who can't read the menu in restaurants are going to be in their cars driving home at the same time I am.

My eyes are so bad that I can't read menus anymore. I have to order from the pictures on the menu. One time I ordered the front of the restaurant.

My dad would never admit his eyes were failing. He'd say, "Son, I can look you right in the face and tell you that my eyesight is as good as ever." I'd have to say, "Pop. I'm over here."

Everything goes when you get older. I asked my grandfather if he'd like me to read the paper to him. He said, "What?"

My grandfather was an excellent marksman well into his eighties. His only problem was that he couldn't read the No Hunting signs.

Everything goes when you get older. I can't read newspaper print anymore. I can still see the pictures, but I can't remember who the people are.

Failing eyesight is Mother Nature's way of slowing us down as we grow older. "Why should you spend so much time reading today," she says, "when you won't remember most of it tomorrow anyway?"

I don't understand Mother Nature. How come when we get older our eyes start to fail but we can still smell as good as ever?

One time, my eyes were so bloodshot that I could watch a lovely sunset at noon.

FORGETFUL

There are three signs of old age: loss of memory . . . I forget the other two.—*Red Skelton*

Nothing is more responsible for the good old days than a bad memory.
—*Robert Benchley*

Am I forgetful? Last night I forgot the Alamo.—*Henny Youngman*

When I was younger I could remember anything, whether it happened or not. But I am getting old and soon I shall remember only the latte.
—*Mark Twain*

The short memories of the American voters is what keeps our politicians in office.—*Will Rogers*

I have a poor memory for names, but I never remember a face.
—*W. C. Fields*

. . .

My memory is starting to go. I locked the keys in my car the other day. Fortunately, I had forgotten to get out first.

The memory is not the first thing to go. It's just that when it goes, you forget about all the other things that went before it.

I've forgotten more about memory loss than you'll ever know.

There are some good things about having a bad memory. Like last week I threw myself a surprise party.
. . . Then I forgot to go.

I have trouble remembering faces. I left mine at home four times last week.

When I got home my wife said, "Did you remember to get milk? Did you pick up the dry cleaning? Did you get the car washed?" I not only forgot those things; I forgot I was married.

There's a strange thing about memory. Damned if I can remember what it is.

I can remember things from years ago, but I can't remember what I had for breakfast this morning. Wait a minute! I forgot to have breakfast this morning.

I went to see a new doctor. He said, "That'll be $25 in advance." I paid him and told him I had a terrible short-term memory. He said, "That'll be $25 in advance."

My doctor prescribed pills for my memory. I'm supposed to take one three times a day, if I can remember where they are.

My brother's memory is just as bad as mine. We both think we're an only child.

 **DIETS**

I've been on a constant diet for the last two decades. I've lost a total of 789 pounds. By all accounts, I should be hanging from a charm bracelet.—*Erma Bombeck*

My wife is a light eater. As soon as it's light, she starts eating.
—*Henny Youngman*

I used to have a great big barrel chest . . . but that's all behind me now.
—*Bob Hope*

I once went on a three-week diet and lost twenty-one days.
—*Jack E. Leonard*

I found there was only one way to look thin—hang out with fat people.
—*Rodney Dangerfield*

. . .

They have a new diet now where you eat nothing but garlic and onions. Everybody stays so far away from you that from a distance you look thinner.

I'm on a diet now that guarantees I'll lose a pound a day.
I'll say good-bye now because by Christmas I'll be gone completely.
. . . If you stay on this diet long enough, you'll need
staples to hold your socks up.

My uncle once went on a total seafood diet. He was doing pretty well, too, until he drowned one day trying to get lunch.

My wife came home one day and said, "Look, honey, I lost 15 pounds." I said, "If you look behind you, you'll find them."
—*Slappy White*

You know you should go on a diet when you buy something marked "one size fits all" and your name is printed on the label as one of the exceptions.

Some of the hamburgers they serve in fast-food restaurants are very thin. If you hold them up to the light, you can read the menu through them.

Some of those snack foods have so many chemicals in them you can't even buy them without a prescription.
. . . I compromise. I buy them, but I keep them in my medicine cabinet.

Our lemonade today is made up of nothing but chemicals. The only place you can get real lemonade is in furniture polish.
. . . Our dining-room table eats better than we do.

They serve food full of chemicals. I looked at the trash cans behind a fast-food restaurant. Fake flies were buzzing around them.

VEGETABLES

The local groceries are all out of broccoli, loccoli.—*Roy Blount, Jr.*

I said to my son, "Finish up all your meat, and you'll grow up and be just like Daddy." Since then he only eats vegetables.—*Rodney Dangerfield*

A vegetarian is a person who won't eat anything that can have children.
—*David Brenner*

• • •

194

My mother used to say, "There are places in this world where people are going to bed hungry." I would say, "Do you really think sending them cauliflower would change that?"

A vegetarian is someone who doesn't eat meat and looks funny at people who do.

Vegetables are of less importance than meat. Do you think people would really care if lima beans got tangled up in the tuna nets?

To me, vegetables are not a food; they're a food accessory.

If you really wanted people to eat something, would you name it succotash?

After a minor accident, one driver said, "If I weren't a priest, I'd chew your ear off." The other driver said, "Then we're equal. I'm a vegetarian."

I heard one vegetarian say, "Boy, I'm so hungry I could eat a horseradish."

Technically, the potato is not a vegetable. It's something you push the vegetables against when you're trying to get them on your fork.

Spoken by the lone vegetarian in a cannibal tribe: "No thanks, I'll just munch on his clothing."

There's one thing you very rarely hear said about vegetables: "It tastes a little bit like chicken."

My mom had a unique way of trying to get me to eat my vegetables. She'd say, "You eat every single thing on your plate, or you'll be sent to bed without your supper."

. . . And I was so dumb, it worked.

EXERCISE

I take my exercise acting as pallbearer at the funerals of those who exercised regularly.—*Mark Twain*

I am pushing 60—that's enough exercise for me.—*Mark Twain*

My wife went to one of those gymnasiums and lost 37 pounds. One of those machines tore her leg off.—*Slappy White*

I exercise daily to keep my figure. I keep patting my hand against the bottom of my chin. It works, too—I have the thinnest fingers in town. —*Totie Fields*

. . .

I don't exercise at all. I figure if God meant for us to touch our toes, He would have put them farther up our body.

I don't want a perfect body. I've had this one for so long, I've grown attached to it.

Some runners in our neighborhood get up and go out jogging at 4:30 in the morning. If I'm ever up at that time of day, I want to be coming home.

There are so many joggers out on the streets in the mornings that cars have to use the sidewalks.

If God wanted us to run down the street, He would have made us with turn signals.

You have to be careful about jogging. The doctor told a neighbor of mine that he should jog three miles every morning. Last we heard from him, he was in Pittsburgh.

I quit smoking. I feel better, I smell better, and it's safer to drink from old beer cans—*Roseanne Barr*

People are so rude to smokers. You'd think they'd try to be nicer to people who are dying.—*Roseanne Barr*

I smoke cigars because at my age if I don't have something to hang onto I might fall down.—*George Burns*

I know it's very easy to give up smoking because I've tried it so often. —*Mark Twain*

I never smoke to excess—that is, I smoke in moderation, only one cigar at a time.—*Mark Twain*

. . .

A lot of people are getting very militant against smokers. The warning on the pack now says, "Smoking may be injurious to your health. The person sitting next to you may hit you with a stick."

You've heard the expression "Where there's smoke, there's fire"?
That's been changed to "Where there's smoke, there's someone nearby
making a face and calling you a dirty name."

They don't allow smoking in most restaurants now. In fact, some even
frown on customers ordering anything well done.

Restaurants have smaller and smaller smoking sections now. I know one
where smoking is only allowed in the kitchen oven that's not being used.

Los Angeles restaurants are getting very strict against smoking.
They have a smoking section, but it's in Oxnard.

Smokers on airplanes are now getting desperate. On one flight, I saw a
guy who was trying to inhale the little picture of a cigarette on the No
Smoking sign.

On long flights now, if an engine starts smoking, the passengers don't get
mad. They get jealous.

They may have to have two masks available on planes from now
on—one filled with oxygen, the other filled with nicotine.

BLESS OUR HAPPY HOME

# HOUSEWIVES

I don't like to be called "housewife." . . . I prefer "domestic goddess."
—*Roseanne Barr*

My wife does wonderful things with leftovers—she throws them out.
—*Herb Shriner*

. . .

You can always tell the housewives from the sweethearts in restaurants. The woman buttering six pieces of bread and passing them clockwise around the table . . . housewife.

Mom put so much starch in everything. I remember one time I sneezed and cut my nose on the handkerchief.
. . . One night, my brother fell out of bed and broke his pajamas.

Try this. Leave the dishes undone, the clothes unwashed, throw trash and garbage all over the house. Then when your husband asks what you've been doing all day, say, "Here it is; I didn't do it."

The only question a man asks after "Will you marry me?" is "What's for dinner?"

It all evens out. Some women subtract five years from their age, but being a housewife adds ten.

Housewife is a profession, just like being a doctor or a lawyer. However, if you have several children, it's more like being an Indian chief.

Housewife is a very important profession. If it weren't for them we'd all be up to our armpits in dirty laundry.

... eating off paper plates.

... and never knowing which shirt goes with which pair of trousers.

MAN AROUND THE HOUSE

My husband is so useless that it's hard for me to be romantic with him. I get down on the floor next to him and say, "If you love me, blink your eyes."—*Phyllis Diller*

I'm an ordinary sort of fellow—42 around the chest, 42 around the waist, 96 around the golf course, and a nuisance around the house.
—*Groucho Marx*

. . .

People say it's nice to have a man around the house.
Not my husband—he's just something else that has to be dusted.

My husband does absolutely nothing around the house. I get the feeling I married a knickknack.

Asking my husband to do something is like talking to the walls, except the walls are standing up.

My husband hasn't mowed the front lawn in so long that the only way the mailman can get to the front door is to swing on a vine.

My husband does absolutely nothing around the house. It's like being married to a giant Tinkertoy.

My husband is the world's greatest procrastinator. At our wedding, the minister said, "You may now kiss the bride." My husband said, "Tomorrow."

My husband does absolutely nothing around the house. I searched all over him for a cord. I figured, maybe you have to plug him in.

My husband is embarrassing. All he ever does is sleep. Sometimes I smear him with grease and slide him under the car just to fool the neighbors.

My husband watches so much football on the weekends that his skin is starting to break out in AstroTurf.

My husband spends a lot of time sleeping on the floor. We thought he was missing once, then we discovered we had just carpeted over him.

HOUSE WORK

I said to my wife, "Where do you want to go for our anniversary?" She said, "I want to go somewhere I've never been before." I said, "Try the kitchen."—*Henny Youngman*

When my husband comes home, if the kids are still alive, I figure I've done my job.—*Roseanne Barr*

When Sears comes out with a riding vacuum cleaner, then I'll clean the house.—*Roseanne Barr*

I hate housework. You make the beds, you do the dishes—and six months later you have to start all over again.—*Joan Rivers*

Housework can kill you if done right.—*Erma Bombeck*

Cleaning your house before the kids have stopped growing is like shoveling the walk before it stops snowing.—*Phyllis Diller*

My mama was afraid to leave dirty dishes in the sink overnight. If a burglar broke in, she would have been embarrassed.—*Sam Levenson*

. . .

When my wife came back from vacation, I knew she'd be mad at the mess the house was in. So I had the kids make up a sign that said: "Welcome home, Mommy!" And we hung it where the dining room used to be.

Our house is such a mess that the termites tried to have us exterminated.

My house is such a mess that the neighbors got a petition up against us. Now we all have to wipe our feet before going out.

The walls in our house are half-clean. Our neighbor takes care of the side that faces her.

I won't say my house is a mess, but have you ever seen a fly land on a cloud of dust?

My kids always leave the bathroom a mess. When they take a bath, they leave a ring around the room.

A lot of people think our bathroom has green carpeting in it. That's moss.

My son has a toy boat that he takes in the bathtub with him. It has done more harm than the real Battleship Missouri. That's because I have never accidentally sat down on the real Battleship Missouri.

I always make my children clean their own room. It's good discipline for them, and besides, I'm two years behind in cleaning the rest of the house.

Last week I went into my son's room and found a big, hairy clump of dirt. It was a friend helping him with his homework.

My son collects all kinds of junk—and fast. The first time I cleaned his room, I found the previous owners trying to find their way out.

My daughter's room is crammed full of stuffed animals. If you accidentally fall down in there, you could be cushioned to death.

COOKING

Me, a cook? I always threatened my children with, "If you don't shape up, you go to bed with dinner."—*Erma Bombeck*

I miss my wife's cooking—as often as I can.—*Henny Youngman*

I know I'm a lousy cook, but I never realized how bad until the other night when I caught the dog calling Chicken Delight.—*Joan Rivers*

I'll give you an idea of how bad my cooking is. Last Christmas the family chipped in together and bought me an oven that flushes.—*Phyllis Diller*

My wife's cooking is so bad that I went in the kitchen once and saw a cockroach eating a Tums.—*Slappy White*

Her favorite dessert recipe begins: "Take the juice from one bottle of Pepto Bismol. . . ."

His specialty is dumplings with the accent on the "dump."

Her cooking keeps flies away better than a shelf no-pest strip.

If you ever want to get revenge on the ants, bring some of his cooking to your next picnic.

Her cooking melts in your mouth. Oh, it may take two or three days, but it melts in your mouth.

His cooking is so bad that his garbage disposal has an ulcer.

Her cooking is so bad that the silverware in her house is imprinted with the Surgeon General's warning.

She's not a real good cook. She can take even the most inexpensive piece of meat and turn it into a lethal weapon.

He asked the family to buy him a chef's hat. They got him a black hood.

I'm a pretty bad cook. If I had cooked the first Thanksgiving meal for the Indians, General Custer might be alive today.

I'll never forget my first meal as a young bride. My husband won't either. He's still being treated for it.

The family knows how dangerous my cooking is. Why else would grace last 45 minutes?

I don't mind my wife serving leftovers once in a while, but from World War II?

My wife is such a bad cook that we have cold cereal for breakfast every morning. She prepares it the night before.

My wife's cooking is so bad that we have holes in our screen door where the flies go out.

One time I saw her give the leftovers to the dog. And the dog gave them to the cat.

Nobody wants to eat her food. In her kitchen, the flies swat themselves.

When she serves the family fried chicken, the chicken is the only lucky one at the table.

KITCHEN APPLIANCES

There is such a buildup of crud in my oven, there is only room to bake a single cupcake.—*Phyllis Diller*

Our toaster works on either AC or DC, but not on bread. It has two settings—too soon or too late.—*Sam Levenson*

Our kitchen had an electric dishwasher, an electric can opener, an electric garbage disposal. . . . My wife said, "There's so many appliances in here I

don't have room to sit down." I bought her an electric chair.
—*Henny Youngman*

My wife forgot this year that she has a microwave oven. You ever eat
Thanksgiving dinner at seven in the morning?—*Robert Orben*

My wife gets mixed up with all the gadgets in the kitchen. Yesterday she
tried to defrost the stove.—*Milton Berle*

Sure my mother had an automatic garbage disposal. She could
detect unerringly when you planned to go out, and put the garbage
bag in your hand.—*Sam Levenson*

We got a new garbage disposal—my brother-in-law. He'll eat anything.
—*Henny Youngman*

This guy just invented a new microwave television set. He can watch 60
Minutes in twelve seconds.—*Milton Berle*

APPLIANCE SALESMAN: You'll like this range. For instance, you put in a
roast, you set the oven control, then you go out all day. When you come
home at night, the roast is done.
GRACIE: Haven't you got one where I don't have to go out?—*Gracie
Allen*

. . .

We have a toaster at home that we got from a bank. Every day at three
o'clock it stops working.

We have a toaster that we got from a bank. It toasts the bread all right,
but you have to fill out a withdrawal slip to get it to pop up.

I'm not real good in the kitchen. I had to shop all over town for a

Cuisinart with training wheels.

We have so many appliances in our kitchen that when we have breakfast, all the traffic lights in our town stop working.

We have a new Cuisinart that does everything in the kitchen. It even cries over spilt milk.

My dad makes his morning coffee in the microwave. Instant coffee is not fast enough for him.

Microwave ovens are so great. Thanks to them, we can now have heartburn without having to wait for it.

Modern appliances are great. Our new toaster has four different dials on it, which means it has 9,999 different ways to burn toast.

Our new juicer makes juice from anything. This morning I had a glass of toast.

We have a self-cleaning oven in our kitchen. Big deal! We've had a cat like that for years.

I often wonder: where did people hang their children's drawings before the refrigerator was invented?

You can't put plastic in the dishwasher, metal in the microwave, utensils

in the garbage disposal. There are so many rules in the kitchen that we find it safer to eat out.

I make a peanut-butter sandwich in the microwave oven. It sticks to the roof of your mouth faster.

I don't like cooking in the microwave. It just means you have to do the dishes that much sooner.

The microwave oven is probably the greatest time-saving device since telling my husband to stay out of the kitchen.

Three of the greatest kitchen time-savers are the self-cleaning oven, the self-defrosting refrigerator, and the self-cooking husband.

We have so many appliances in the kitchen that I feel out of place there unless I'm plugged in.

Years ago, I remember my father coming home from work and saying to my mother, "I'm sick and tired of you bending over a hot stove in the kitchen all day. Straighten up."

Everything in our kitchen is automatic and has a timer. My wife could leave me tomorrow and I'd still eat well through next Tuesday.

CALL THE HANDY MAN

You can tell that a husband isn't handy when he asks the man next door how to get blood off a saw.—*Milton Berle*

. . .

You put a hammer in my husband's hand, and you've put together two things with roughly the same intelligence.

My husband has a can of nails in the garage with a little note on the top that reads: "Pointy side toward wall."

The only time my husband has ever joined two pieces of wood together was when he accidentally hit himself in the head with a 2x4.

My husband is no handyman. I asked him to hang a picture for me. He tied a piece of rope around it and kicked a chair from under it.

My husband is not good with tools unless it happens to be a beer-can opener.

My husband is dangerous on handyman projects. He has a tool box that's filled to the top—with a screwdriver, a hammer, and Band-Aids.

My husband is such a dangerous handyman that his toolbox has a siren on it.

I just had my kitchen redone. It started out when I asked my husband to hang the curtains.

My husband tried to fix our plumbing himself. We now get our water by mail.

My husband somehow got our plumbing mixed up with the electricity. Now every time I take a shower, all our lights go out.
. . . What's worse than that, our television set leaks.

 # DECORATING

My wife is an interior decorator. She wants to get rid of me because I clash with the drapes.—*Morey Amsterdam*

When I was a kid, we were evicted so often we had to buy curtains that matched the sidewalks.—*Milton Berle*

. . .

Our living room has striped furniture with polka-dot wallpaper. It doesn't look pretty, but our company never stays too long.

We had our whole house done in stripes. Good fashion sense prevented the kids from getting the measles.

We had our bedroom and bathroom done entirely in plush, white carpeting. If I nick myself shaving, I have to go to the neighbors' house to bleed.

Everything in our house is neutral except my mother- in-law.

We did our family room entirely in plaids. First thing that happened was my son's pet chameleon had a
nervous breakdown.

We wanted a house that looked "lived in," so we bought all our furniture from the YMCA.

We decorated our den entirely in black. First thing I lost was my bowling ball.

We decorated our house in such authentic earth tones that now every August the leaves fall off our dining room table.

I told the decorator I wanted the home to "be me." She added a bay window.

I told the decorator I wanted an office that reflected my work habits. He took out the desk and put in a daybed.

FAMILY TIES & BINDS

Marriage

Childhood

Children

Relatives

Bachelors

Dating

Pets

MARRIAGE

My husband has always felt that marriage and a career don't mix; that's why he's never worked. —*Phyllis Diller*

I should have known something was wrong with my first wife when I brought her home to meet my parents and they approved.—*Woody Allen*

My wife is an immature woman. I would be home in the bathroom taking a bath, and my wife would walk in whenever she felt like it and sink my boats.—*Woody Allen*

Did you ever notice when a guy opens a car door for his wife, either the car is new or the wife is.—*Woody Woodbury*

I haven't spoken to my wife in weeks—I didn't want to interrupt her. —*Henny Youngman*

My wife has a slight impediment in her speech—every once in a while she stops to breathe.—*Henny Youngman*

Fang and I are always fighting. When we get up in the morning, we don't kiss; we touch gloves.—*Phyllis Diller*

Marriage is the alliance of two people, one of whom never remembers birthdays and the other who never forgets them.—*Ogden Nash*

My wife loves to argue. When I said, "I do," she said, "Oh no you don't."

A good marriage lasts forever and a bad one seems to.

Most people get married because they're hopelessly in love. Then it's a toss-up which lasts longer—the love or the hopelessness.

When we celebrated our 50th wedding anniversary, I said, "Honey, it just doesn't seem like 50 years." She said, "Speak for yourself."

Some people say they don't believe in marriage because it's only a piece of paper. So is money, but we all believe in that.

EVE: Adam, are you seeing another woman?
ADAM: What do you think —I'm made of ribs?

 **CHILDHOOD**

I had a very funny childhood. My mother used to tell me so much about the birds and the bees that it took me years and years to get interested in girls.—*Jack E. Leonard*

Each kid nowadays has his own TV, hi-fi, and air- conditioning. Why, when I was a boy, the only time we had air-conditioning was when my mother blew on the minestrone.—*Danny Thomas*

It is good to obey the rules when you're young so that you'll have the strength to break them when you're old.—*Mark Twain*

Childhood is a time of rapid changes. Between the ages of twelve and seventeen, a parent can age 30 years.—*Sam Levenson*

One day my father took me aside and left me there.—*Jackie Vernon*

Childhood is a time of life when you have no cares, no worries, no problems,no responsibilities, no money. It sounds a lot like my Uncle Charlie's adulthood.

The first thing that happened in my childhood was that the doctor slapped my bottom and made me cry. Then he gave my father the bill and made *him* cry.

I don't remember if my childhood was happy or not. I was only a kid at the time.

I had a very moving childhood. My parents kept moving without telling me where they were going.

There were always a lot of happy children around our house, which annoyed me. I was an only child.

During my childhood I created imaginary playmates. Then one night they stole all my toys.

This friend of mine had a sheltered childhood. His parents told his teacher, "If he acts up in school, just punish the child next to him."

My mother would try to rock me to sleep as a child, but I kept dodging the rocks.

Some people ask me: "If you had your childhood to live over again, would you do it?" I doubt it—I'm fresh out of diapers.

CHILDREN

Home nowadays is a place where part of the family waits till the rest of the family brings the car back.—*Earl Wilson*

Any mother with half a skull knows that when Daddy's little boy becomes Mommy's little boy, the kid is so wet that he's treading water. —*Erma Bombeck*

The last thing my kids ever did to earn money was lose their baby teeth.—*Phyllis Diller*

My kid said, "Daddy, Mommy said you should take me to the zoo." I said, "If the zoo wants you, let them come and get you."—*Slappy White*

Reprimand your child regularly every day. You may not know why, but the kid does.—*Harry Hershfield*

Never raise your hand to your children. It leaves your midsection unprotected.—*Fred Allen*

How times have changed! Remember 30 years ago, when a juvenile delinquent was a kid with an overdue library book?—*Henny Youngman*

I had to go to school to see my kid's guidance counselor. They told me my kid was out; he'd be back in one to three years.—*Rodney Dangerfield*

I won't say our kids are bad, but we had to turn down one baby-sitter because she didn't own a crash helmet.

Some of those video games kids play today are so violent. Little girls don't want dolls now unless they blow up other dolls.

A little boy asked his friend, "How old are you?" The friend said, "I don't know. Four or five." The older boy asked, "Do you dream about girls?" The friend said, "No." The boy said, "You're four."

During the whole drive to our summer vacation, the kids kept asking, "Are we there yet?" Once we arrived they kept asking, "When can we go home?"

RELATIVES

I slept in the same bed with six brothers. We had a bed wetter. It took us three years to find out who it was.—*Bob Hope*

My sister just had a baby. I can't wait to find out if I'm an aunt or an uncle.—*Gracie Allen*

I grew up with six brothers. That's how I learned to dance— waiting to get into the bathroom.—*Bob Hope*

My brother is very superstitious. He won't work any week that has a Friday in it.—*Milton Berle*

My crazy brother-in-law! I wish he would learn a trade; that way we'd know what kind of work he's out of.—*Henny Youngman*

GEORGE: This family of yours—they all lived together?
GRACIE: Yes, my father, my uncle, my cousin, my brother, and my nephew used to sleep in one bed, and my—
GEORGE: I'm surprised your grandfather didn't sleep with them.
GRACIE: Oh, he did, but he died and they made him get up.
—*George Burns and Gracie Allen*

. . .

They call it a family tree because, if you look hard enough, you'll always find some sap in it.

My parents had a large family. The only way they could afford to feed us all was to start a game of hide-and-seek right before dinner.

There were so many kids in diapers in our family that our house was the only one on the block with a rainbow over it.

My mother always told me that lima beans would put hair on my chest. I don't know how she got my sister to eat them.

My little brother was a mean, vicious child. He would always hit me back.

He has to talk constantly. Once he had laryngitis—he just moved his lips and hired a ventriloquist to travel around with him.

My little brother used to break all my toys, lose parts of all my games, and louse up all my coloring books. I could never catch him at it because I was in my college classes all day.

My brother won't eat any seafood at all. If he comes back in the next life as a pelican, the only time he'll eat is if a cow drowns.

My brother likes all his meat to be cooked extra well done. He doesn't like it to come with a baked potato; he likes it to come with an arson inspector.

My Uncle Newt is as strong as a horse. We just wish he had the l.Q. of one.

I feel sorry for my poor, goofy uncle. We can't let him have anything sharp—like a mind.

He's very goofy. When the cuckoo bird comes out of the clock every hour, he tries to pull my uncle back in with him.

BACHELORS

A bachelor believes that one can live as cheaply as two.—*Milton Berle*

A bachelor is a guy who hasn't let a woman pin anything on him since he wore diapers.—*Milton Berle*

I belong to Bridegrooms Anonymous. Whenever I feel like getting married, they send over a lady in a housecoat and hair curlers to burn my toast for me.—*Dick Martin*

Some say a bachelor is a man who has never made the same mistake once.

Men are bachelors by choice. Sometimes it's their choice; sometimes it's the choice of the women they meet.

Being a bachelor is tough; you have to hog your own covers.

Remaining a bachelor is one way of keeping all that alimony money for yourself.

When it comes to marriage, a bachelor is a man who gets cold feet and no one to keep them warm in bed.

A bachelor never knows the joy of wedded bliss, never knows the joy of having children, and never knows the joy of rearing a family. But he does know the joy of never knowing those other joys.

Being a bachelor means you can mow the lawn when you want to.

A married man is the head of his household, but a bachelor has total control of his own television remote-control device.

 # DATING

I have no self-confidence. When girls tell me yes, I tell them to think it over.—*Rodney Dangerfield*

Will Rogers said he never met a man he didn't like. But then, Will Rogers never had to date one.—*Linda Perret*

I don't date women my own age—there are no women my own age.
—*George Burns*

The only thing he ever takes out on a moonlit night is his upper plate.
—*Fred Allen*

I asked my date what she wanted to drink. She said, "Oh, I guess I'll have champagne." I said, "Guess again."—*Slappy White*

I went on a first date with one girl. She ran into a guy she used to know. She introduced me to him. She said, "Steve, this is Rodney. Rodney, this is good-bye."—*Rodney Dangerfield*

One woman I was dating said, "Come on over, there's nobody home." I went over—nobody was home.—*Rodney Dangerfield*

. . .

My daughter brought home a date who was so ugly, I said, "You can marry him if you want, but I'm not going to the wedding unless he agrees to wear a veil, too."

Falling in love is like buying a new car—and marriage is the first scratch.

HER FATHER: Have my daughter home by midnight.
HER DATE: Why? Does she turn into a pumpkin?

I used to date our town librarian. I asked her to marry me once, and she said, "Sssshhhh!"

I took the daughter of the school librarian to the Junior Prom. If I didn't have her back by midnight, I got fined a nickel a minute.
. . . I not only had to get her home on time, but I had to return her to the same shelf from which I picked her up.

I've got a friend who'll chase anything in a skirt, which is why our school band got rid of their bagpipe uniforms.

PETS

I love a dog. He does nothing for political reasons.—*Will Rogers*

If you pick up a starving dog and make him prosper, he will not bite you. This is the principal difference between a man and a dog.—*Mark Twain*

I have nothing against dogs. I just hate rugs that go squish-squish.
—*Phyllis Diller*

A boy can learn a lot from a dog: obedience, loyalty, and the importance of turning around three times before lying down.—*Robert Benchley*

. . .

I have bad luck with pets. I had a wooden hobbyhorse when I was a kid. It kicked me in the head.

I once had a dog that was so smart that when we went to obedience school, I was the one on the leash.

I once had a dog that really believed he was man's best friend. He kept borrowing money from me.

I just taught my cocker spaniel how to beg. The other day he came home with $4.37.

The worst thing I ever did was teach my poodle how to beg. Once he learned, he joined the Hare Krishnas, and now he spends all his time at the airport.

We have a very large family dog. He doesn't permit us to sit on the sofa.

This guy said, "Don't worry about the dog. His bark is worse than his bite." I hope he never barks at me, because his bite required fourteen stitches.

GOOD MORNING & GOOD NIGHT

Waking Up

Breakfast

Bedtime

Sleep

Dreams

Snoring

Insomnia

WAKING UP

The early bird would never catch the worm if the dumb worm slept late.—*Milton Berle*

You should see the way my wife looks in the morning. She ran after the garbage man and said, "Am I too late for the garbage?" He said, "No, jump in."—*Henny Youngman*

I tried giving up coffee in the morning, but I noticed something: When I woke up, I didn't.—*Milton Berle*

If your eyes hurt after you drink coffee in the morning, you have to take the spoon out of the cup.—*Norm Crosby*

Nowadays I'm beginning to have morning sickness. I'm not having a baby—it's just that I'm sick of morning.—*Phyllis Diller*

Men are very strange. When they wake up in the morning they want things like toast. I don't have these recipes.—*Elayne Boosler*

Last week I noticed my gums were shrinking. I was brushing my teeth with Preparation H.—*Rodney Dangerfield*

. . .

There is no such thing as a good morning. They all begin with waking up.

I'm such a grouch in the morning that not even the milkman will come near the house. He mails us our milk.

I'm very grouchy when I wake up in the morning. The safest way to get me out of bed is to step on my back and pick me up by the claws.

I must look a mess when I get up. My wife hires a woman to come in once a day and kiss me good morning.

Some people hate waking up and getting out of bed. I enjoy it. I do it three or four times a day.

There are 24 hours in a day. Do you realize that if there were 24 hours and 15 minutes in a day, we could all get enough sleep?

For me, there's one good thing about waking up in the morning: the realization that everything I do for the rest of the day is going to be easier than this.

My mother always used to tell me that the early bird catches the worm. It's probably one of the least appealing incentives for getting out of bed I've ever heard.
. . . If I get out of bed early, I want a better reward than a slimy worm.

I hate to get up in the morning. I like to climb into my water bed and stay there as long as the water does.

I had to get a new alarm clock. It flashes a light, rings a bell, then gives me mouth-to-mouth resuscitation.

My wife said I can have breakfast in bed anytime I want it. All I have to do is sleep in the kitchen.

The first thing I do when I get up in the morning is jump in the shower. Someday I'm going to learn to take my pajamas off first.

My uncle was a farmer, and he only slept late one day in his life—the day the rooster had laryngitis.

BREAKFAST

In England, people actually try to be brilliant at breakfast. Only dull people are brilliant at breakfast.—*Oscar Wilde*

Never work before breakfast. If you have to work before breakfast, eat your breakfast first.—*Josh Billings*

Breakfast cereals that come in the same colors as polyester leisure suits make oversleeping a virtue.—*Fran Lebowitz*

. . .

At my house I enjoy breakfast the most. At other meals, I'm awake enough to know what the food is.

I'm too lazy to make breakfast. I just give the family slices of bread and call it Toast Tartare.

I'm amazed at people who eat a big breakfast. How can you work up an appetite sleeping?

I love the smell of fresh coffee in the morning. That's why I use Maxwell House After-Shave Lotion.

I think if I have a good breakfast, I could go without food for the rest of the day. I think that until about lunchtime.

I don't like cereal that snaps, crackles, and pops in the morning.
I want it to be like me—just sit there and sop up the milk.

I went to a restaurant where three eggs cost $8.95. The waitress said,
"Would you like them scrambled?" I said, "No. At $3 an egg
I want to count them."

Brunch is a meal somewhere between breakfast and lunch. What would
you call a meal you have somewhere around three in the morning?
A midnight sneakfast?

I am a total animal until I've had my first cup of coffee in the morning.
If coffee had never been invented, I could have been Jack the Ripper.

My wife always burns the toast and leaves the eggs runny. I said,
"Tomorrow morning why don't you scramble the bread and pop
the eggs in the toaster?"

I served my wife breakfast in bed the other day. She enjoyed it, then
spent the rest of the day cleaning up the kitchen.

BEDTIME

The amount of sleep required by the average person is about 5 minutes
longer.—*Max Kauffmann*

Any kid will run any errand for you, if you ask at bedtime.—*Red Skelton*

My wife came to bed one night with her hair in curlers and grease on her
face. I didn't know whether to kiss her or play trick-or-treat.
—*Slappy White*

When my wife goes to sleep at night, she packs so much mud on her face, I say, "Good night, swamp!"—*Henny Youngman*

It's true Fang and I fight, but we've never gone to bed mad. Of course, one year we were up for three months.—*Phyllis Diller*

Do you know what it means to come home at night to a woman who'll give you a little love, a little affection, a little tenderness? It means you're in the wrong house, that's what it means.—*Henny Youngman*

I hate it when my foot falls asleep during the day—because then I know it will be up all night.—*Steven Wright*

. . .

Bedtime is not my favorite time of the day. It comes right before my favorite time of the day.

My kid is very good about kissing me goodnight and going up to bed without a fuss. He should be. He does it three, four, five times a night.

For a long time I couldn't close my eyes at night to get to sleep. My wife finally figured out the problem—the drawstring on my pajamas was too tight.

My wife's mad at me because I went to sleep early last night. About 12 feet before I got to the front door.

My wife and I always kiss goodnight. It's like touching gloves before we spend the entire night fighting over the covers.

I'm not really good at math, but I have trouble figuring out why my better half requires three-fourths of the covers at night.

Every night, when I go to bed, I kiss my wife good night and my covers good-bye.

My wife always steals my covers during the night. What bothers me most about this is that we have twin beds.

My wife says, "Why do you have to go to sleep so early every night?" I say, "I'm anxious to dream about you."

My wife and I always settle any disagreements before going to bed at night. Then we try to fall asleep real fast before the next fight starts.

I always set my alarm before going to bed at night. It gives me something to ignore in the morning.

My uncle invented a coffee that makes you see double. If it keeps you up at night, you'll have company.

SLEEP

I woke up and my girl asked if I slept well. I said, "No, I made a couple of mistakes."—*Steven Wright*

I have never taken any exercise—except sleep and rest.—*Mark Twain*

I bought one of those tapes to teach you Spanish in your sleep. During the night, the tape skipped. The next day I could only stutter in Spanish.—*Steven Wright*

My wife missed her nap today. Slept right through it.—*Henny Youngman*

I just passed the age of 30, and you get a little introspective once you

pass 30. Like I'm beginning to appreciate the value of a nap.
—*Marsha Warfield*

. . .

I don't think humans were meant to walk upright—because it tires me out so quickly.

Sleep is probably the most fun you can have in this life without being awake to enjoy it.

I sleep a lot. The only exercise I get is tossing and turning.

The only way sleep could be more enjoyable for me is if I could find a way to make money from it.

My hobby is napping. It's not only fun; it's inexpensive.

Some people say they can't sleep at night. That may be true, although I've never been awake to hear them say it.

I love sleep. To me, anything done with both eyes open already has two strikes against it.

Horses can sleep standing up. Of course, if you pulled a milk wagon all day, you probably could, too.

Do you know what I call people who get 8 hours' sleep a night? Amateurs.

Sharks never sleep. That's why you'll never catch one wearing pajamas.

Sleep is meant to refresh, rejuvenate, and revitalize us, so we'll be ready for another good night's sleep tomorrow night.

DREAMS

I had a terrible dream yesterday. I dreamed I was awake all night.
—*Milton Berle*

This morning I woke up from a dream and went right into a daydream.
—*Steven Wright*

He dreamed he was eating shredded wheat and woke up to find the mattress half gone.—*Fred Allen*

You know a man is getting old when his dreams about girls are reruns.
—*Henny Youngman*

My aunt said to her husband, "Max, last night I dreamed you bought me a fur coat." Her husband said, "In your next dream, wear it in good health."—*Henny Youngman*

I just had a wonderful dream. I dreamed the Joneses were trying to keep up with *me.*—*Henny Youngman*

I had a terrible dream last night. I dreamed that my girl and Sophia Loren had a fight over me. And my girl won.—*Joe E. Lewis*

• • •

One thing I like about dreams: you have to be asleep to have them.

Dreams are like sermons in church. They're better if you sleep right through them.

I was having such a terrible dream the other night that it woke me up. Then I realized my real life was worse.

I dreamed I was stuck on a deserted island with three gorgeous women. The sad part was, I was a palm tree.

My wife woke me last night and said, "I'm having a terrible dream." I said, "Ask for your money back."

Last week I dreamed the entire night that I was running from people who were chasing me. When I woke up, I was not only covered with perspiration, but I was somewhere in Ohio.

I think I watch too much television. Last night, my dreams kept being interrupted for commercials.

I do watch too much TV. I had a dream the other night, and at the end of it, a list of credits rolled by.

Television has definitely influenced me. I'm searching now for a stand-up comedian to star in my dreams.

The other night I dreamed I was a Boy Scout who won a knot-tying contest. When I woke up I couldn't get the drawstring on my pajamas undone.

The other night I dreamed I was a shark who swam in oceans all over the world. When I woke up, boy, were my gills tired.

I dreamed the other night that I was a soldier in Custer's last stand. When I woke up my pajamas were at half-mast.

SNORING

There ain't no way to find out why a snorer can't hear himself snore.
—*Mark Twain*

. . .

My spouse snores so loudly, the people in my dreams complain that they can't hear one another talk.

My husband says, "How can you prove that I snore so loudly?" I say, "Look, those windows weren't broken when we went to bed last night."

Snoring is nature's way of saying, "Hey, everybody wake up and look at me. I'm sleeping."

My husband snores so loudly I think he studied sleeping under Harley-Davidson.

There's only one sure cure for snoring: insomnia.

My husband's snoring is not always so bad. Sometimes it drowns out the noise of passing trains.

I've discovered that a glass of cool water can stop my husband's snoring—if I pour it down the front of his pajamas.

Some scientists say a tennis ball sewn into the back of the pajamas can stop snoring. I'd rather just whack the snorer on the head with the racket.

My husband's snoring is so bad we have to sleep in shifts. I try to sneak in a nap while he's inhaling.

My husband's snoring saves me a fortune in beauty treatments. He snores so loudly that it curls my hair.
. . . and my toes.

My husband's snoring sounds like the mating call of the elephant seal. Every morning he gets love letters from the Pacific Ocean.

INSOMNIA

A good cure for insomnia is: Get plenty of sleep.—*W. C. Fields*

Don't wake him up; he's got insomnia. He's trying to sleep it off.
—*Chico Marx*

Life is something that happens when you can't get to sleep.
—*Fran Lebowitz*

The doctor says I might have insomnia, but I'm not going to lose any sleep over it.

I wish someone would find a cure for my insomnia. I dreamed about that all last night.

My uncle hasn't slept a wink in about three years. He's a great guy to buy used pajamas from.

My uncle has a very bad case of insomnia. He goes to flop houses and then can't flop.

My uncle's under a lot of stress because of medical reasons. He has insomnia and sleeping sickness at the same time.

UNCLE: I've got amnesia so bad I haven't slept in 5 weeks.
ME: No, Uncle. *Insomnia* is when you can't sleep.
UNCLE: Oh, I *can* sleep. I just keep forgetting to.

The good news is that my uncle finally got over his insomnia. The bad news is that he was driving on the interstate at the time.

I had an appointment with a doctor who promised he could cure my insomnia, but he overslept.

Look at the bright side of insomnia—it's a great cure for snoring.

My doctor can't cure my insomnia, but he does the next best thing. He tells me how well he slept.

I think I might be getting over my insomnia. The other day my foot fell asleep.

I've had insomnia for 7 weeks, and finally last night I fell asleep. My wife woke me up to tell me the good news.

There are some advantages to having insomnia. Now I know when my husband is stealing the covers.

SCHOOL DAZE

Education

Arithmetic

Dummies

Brains

Graduation

EDUCATION

Everybody is ignorant, only on different subjects. —*Will Rogers*

Training is everything. The peach was once a bitter almond. Cauliflower is nothing but cabbage with a college education. —*Mark Twain*

I never let my schooling interfere with my education. —*Mark Twain*

The teacher told my kid, "An apple a day keeps the doctor away." He said, "What do you got for cops?"—*Rodney Dangerfield*

My education was dismal. I went to a series of schools for mentally disabled teachers.—*Woody Allen*

CHARLIE MCCARTHY: I can't take this schoolwork anymore—
it's driving me nuts.
EDGAR BERGEN: Well, Charlie, I'm sorry, but hard work never killed anyone.
CHARLIE MCCARTHY: Still, there's no use in taking chances.

. . .

I think football games are an important part of college life. In some colleges, it's the only chance the team gets to see the campus.

College football is a money sport. They wanted one kid to drop out of school and sign with the pros, but he couldn't afford the cut in pay.

Spring break from college—that's a riot with school colors.

Of course, you can't blame them. They study hard. After a tough midterm exam, it's relaxing to turn over a car.

Students love Parents' Day. It's a chance to get their money without wasting a stamp.

Parents' Day begins with a scavenger hunt. The parents go to their kid's room, move all the junk around, and see who can be the first one to find their kid.

Education can get you the only thing that really matters in today's world—an assigned parking space.

ARITHMETIC

A teacher asked, "If you had five apples and I asked for one, how many would you have left?" A boy answered, "Five."—*Milton Berle*

I was raised in the days of times tables. We used to recite times tables for company.—*Sam Levenson*

She doesn't understand the concept of Roman numerals. She thought we just fought World War Eleven.—*Joan Rivers*

• • •

My dad says I should study my numbers hard. He says arithmetic is something you can always count on.

PROFESSOR: If you have five apples and I take away four of them, what will you have left?
STUDENT: One apple—to throw at you for taking my other four.

I have a friend who is so bad at arithmetic he has to take off his shoes and socks to count how many fingers he has.

PROFESSOR: If you have 26 cents in one pants pocket and 32 cents in the other, how much money do you have?
STUDENT: None. All my pants have holes in the pockets.

PROFESSOR: What are prime numbers?
BILLY: Numbers that are on television between 8 o'clock and 11 o'clock.

PROFESSOR: What do you get if you multiply 13,362 by 476?
STUDENT: Confused.

TEACHER: If you have 12 cents in one pants pocket and 6 cents in the other pants pocket, what do you have?
BILLY: A lot of trouble—because my mother gave me a dollar and a quarter when I left home for school this morning.

I'm very bad at arithmetic. I can count from 1 to 100, but I have trouble putting the numbers in order.

Our teacher said, "Three men dig a hole in 9 hours. How long would it take six men to dig it?" I said, "Why don't they use the hole the other three guys just dug?"

I've flunked arithmetic three times now. Once more will make it five.

Our teacher said, "What would you get if you divided 7,938 by 143?" I said, "Probably another F in arithmetic."

DUMMIES

In kindergarten, I flunked sand pile.—*Joey Bishop*

You've got the brain of a four-year-old boy, and I bet he was glad to get rid of it.—*Groucho Marx*

One dumb guy was elected dogcatcher. He knew he was supposed to catch dogs—but at what?—*Milton Berle*

My husband Fang is so dumb. I once said, "There's a dead bird," and he looked up.—*Phyllis Diller*

They taught this dumb guy how to run a helicopter. It's up 800 feet. All of a sudden, it falls to the ground. I said to him, "What happened? "He says, "It got chilly up there, so I turned off the fan."—*Henny Youngman*

In San Francisco they have a new dumb mime group. They talk!
—*Henny Youngman*

What's on your mind, if you will allow the overstatement?—*Fred Allen*

• • •

This guy is so dumb that he took his dog to obedience school. The dog passed; he flunked.

I have a friend who is so dumb that when he gets amnesia, he actually gets smarter.

I knew one guy who was so dumb that he had his address tattooed to his forehead. That way, if he got lost, he could mail himself home.

This guy is so lame-brained that he parts his hair in the middle so that he won't have to remember each morning which side he parts it on.

One guy was so dumb that he had to have "left" and "right" tattooed on his toes so that he would know which feet his shoes go on. Now, if he could only learn to read.

One guy was so dumb that he lost his shoes one day because he put them on the wrong feet. Then he couldn't remember whose feet he put them on.

One friend of mine was so stupid he had to take the I.Q. test twice to get it up to a whole number.

Talk about stupid! Someone gave this guy a pair of cuff links. He didn't have a shirt with French cuffs, so he had his wrists pierced.

This guy is stupid. His hobby used to be catching butterflies, but he got tired of digging up worms to use for bait.

I had a friend who was so dumb that he mixed baby powder with water and tried to get a little brother.

I have a friend who is a flower child. He's a blooming idiot.

I asked this guy if he could think on his feet. He said, "Certainly. Who else's feet would I think on?"
. . . He not only thinks on his feet but apparently with them.

This guy is so dumb he thinks Shirley Temple is a synagogue for children.

Someone once explained to this guy that a comet was a star with a tail. He now thinks Lassie is a comet.

 **BRAINS**

I am smart. I know a lot; I just can't think of it.—*Morey Amsterdam*

Smartness runs in my family. When I went to school I was so smart my teacher was in my class for five years.—*Gracie Allen*

You know that horses are smarter than people. You've never heard of a horse going broke betting on people.—*Will Rogers*

It is so simple to be smart. Just think of something stupid to say; then say the opposite.—*Sam Levenson*

Smart is when you believe only half of what you hear. *Brilliant* is when you know which half to believe.—*Robert Orben*

. . .

He's so intelligent. Talking with him is equivalent to passing the bar exam.

When I talk to him, I feel a dunce cap starting to grow out the top of my head.

This friend of mine has a good head on his shoulders. No neck, just a good head.

This guy is brilliant. He could explain Einstein's theory
. . . to Einstein.

This guy uses words that are longer than my resume.

I know this guy who's such a brain. If he doesn't know the answer, there isn't one.

I went to school with a kid who was so smart that the only time he got an answer wrong, they had to go back and change the question.

We had a kid in our class who we used to call The Brain. Not because he was smart, but because he was gray and lumpy and shaped like a big cauliflower.

GRADUATION

A crazy guy ran up to me today and kept yelling, "Call me a doctor! Call me a doctor!" I said, "What's the matter? Are you sick?" He said, "No, I just graduated from medical school." —*Henny Youngman*

My mom and dad were so proud of me when I graduated from high school—so were my wife and kids.

My dad gave me the best advice as they handed me my high-school diploma. He yelled, "Take it and run, Son."

I hated to graduate from high school.
It was ten of the happiest years of my life.

When I graduated from college, I had no idea what I was going to do, but I had a piece of paper that said I knew how to do it.

A college diploma is a piece of paper that says your education is now complete; now it's time to get off your butt and start paying for it.

A young friend of mine wrote: "Dear Mom and Dad, Since I graduated from law school today, I will no longer have to write and ask you for money. Now I know how to demand it."

Another friend wrote: "Dear Mom and Dad, I graduated from medical school, so you no longer have to send me money. Just have your insurance company send it."

I couldn't believe it when I graduated with honors. Neither could the school. That's why they made me retake all the tests.

MY HOMETOWN

Small Town

Dull Town

Crooked Politician

Town Gossip

Village Idiot

Town Drunk

Neat Neighbors

Grouchy Neighbors

Tough Neighborhood

SMALL TOWN

This town was so small they had a fashion show at Sears. No models, they just held open the catalog and the women would point.—*Joan Rivers*

This is a small town. Their 7-Eleven is called 2-Five.—*Joan Rivers*

His hometown is so small, the road map is actual size.—*Milton Berle*

This town was so small, the all-night drugstore closed at noon.
—*Jackie Vernon*

I once played in a town so small that if you went out for a night on the town, it took only half an hour.—*Jack E. Leonard*

I hate small towns because once you've seen the cannon in the park, there's nothing else to do.—*Lenny Bruce*

. . .

Our town was so small it only had two streets in it—Main Street and Not-Main Street.

Our town was so small, to make it look bigger, we put a mirror at one end of it.

Ours used to be a one-horse town, until the horse quit.

Our town was so small that we had to close the public library. Someone tore a few pages out of the book.

Everything was small in our town. Even our sheriff only had room for three points on his badge.

This town was so small, if you sneezed, everybody in town said, "God bless you."

Our town was so small, if two people stopped to talk, it was considered a town meeting.

Our town was so small that the mayor also had to double as the village idiot.. . . He did well in both positions.

All the towns were small where I lived. At our Little League ballpark, each base was in a different county.

The big excitement in my town was to go down to the railroad station and watch them give haircuts.—*Herb Shriner*

A dull town is one in which there's no place to go where you shouldn't be.—*Alexander Woollcott*

His hometown is so dull the drugstore sells picture postcards of other towns. —*Milton Berle*

The only way to have fun in his hometown is to move away. —*Milton Berle*

Our town is so dull that at the annual Fourth of July picnic, we had a firework.

The leader of our local biker club rides a moped.

Our town is so dull that our local newspaper doesn't even have a front page.

In our post office they put up wanted posters of all the people who have books overdue at the library.

Our town is so dull we had one resident who was in a coma for three months. He woke up and hadn't missed a thing.

The most excitement our town had was the heated debate over installing a traffic light on Main Street. It wasn't whether to install it or not; it was over what color the lights should be.

We only have two traffic signs in our town. The first one says "Stop. " The second says "Stop What?"

Even though our town has very little crime, we still have a very efficient police force except when he's not feeling well.

Nothing ever happens in our town. Our town gossip had to hire a writing staff.

Ours is a quiet little town. In fact, one resident sued his next-door neighbor because he claimed his grass was growing too loudly.

The high-school football games draw about 500 people on Friday evenings. They draw a little bit more if the other team shows up.

The biggest spectacle is when someone is going to board the train to leave town. You see, our town doesn't have a train stop.

CROOKED POLITICIAN

He's just the candidate to get our town moving. I know if he wins, I'm moving.—*Milton Berle*

Our town elected a new police chief. His first job was to arrest the old police chief. —*Milton Berle*

The only way to combat criminals is by not voting for them. —*Dayton Allen*

It was hard for me to leave my hometown. . . . covered in tar and feathers as I was. —*Gene Perret*

. . .

He was a crooked politician. To open the Little League each season, instead of throwing out the first ball, he would steal the first base. . . . And he'd keep it.

This politician had his hand out so often his palm was sunburned.

Our town had the most crooked mayor in history. Even the sign in City Hall that directed you to the mayor's office said, "Go down this corridor and under the table."
. . . Yes, the mayor was so crooked, he had his office under a table.
. . . He wanted to be near his money.

Our mayor took all kinds of bribes. When he raised his right hand to take the oath of office, somebody put money in it.

He lived off graft. He was the only mayor I ever saw whose office had an opening in the door for night deposits.

His campaign slogan was: "It's your money. Why give it to a stranger?"

In his office at City Hall, he had the first dollar he ever made framed and hanging on the wall . . . along with the brown paper bag it came in.

But you always knew where to find the mayor. He was always either in his office or in somebody else's pocket.

He would be away from his office for long stretches of time, too—sometimes to 5 years.

Gossip is when you hear something you like about someone you don't.
—*Earl Wilson*

If you can't say something good about someone, sit right here by me.
—*Alice Roosevelt Longworth*

What a talker he is! He could persuade a fish to come out and take a walk with him.—*Mark Twain*

My wife says she doesn't like to repeat gossip, but she says, "What else is there to do with it?"—*Milton Berle*

You can't believe everything you hear, but it's fun to repeat it anyway.
—*Milton Berle*

People loved to spread gossip in our town. It got so bad that the telephone company had to install speed bumps on all the party lines.

Every town has gossip. If you don't hear any, you're it.

Our town had such hot gossip going back and forth over the back fence, that sometimes the fence would catch fire.

One lady in our town spent so much time spreading gossip over the back fence that her tongue had splinters.

We had one lady in town who could spread gossip so fast that they had to paint a racing stripe down her tongue.

This lady was lightning quick and ferocious at spreading rumors. She had a black belt in the English language.

Often she could tell the entire neighborhood what you did before you were done doing it.

This lady tried very hard to keep a secret. In fact, she'd always get ten or twelve people to help her keep it.

She never stopped spreading gossip. Even when she was asleep, the teeth in the glass by her bedside would continue to talk about people.

She was a very mean gossip. She'd go around spreading the truth behind people's backs.

Her philosophy was: if she didn't have anything good to say about a person, she'd say it anyway.

Of course, really juicy gossip is something you wouldn't believe in a million years, but it sure is fun hearing it.

VILLAGE IDIOT

The guy who invented the first wheel was an idiot. The guy who invented the other three—he was a genius.—*Sid Caesar*

Our village idiot bought himself a pet zebra. Named it Spot.
—*Henny Youngman*

. . .

Of course, our town had a village idiot, too. He could never watch *Jeopardy!* unless it came with subtitles.

We had a very unique town idiot. His shoe size and his I.Q. were exactly the same.

This guy was so dumb he could get lost staying home.

One year he went to see Mt. Rushmore and said he wasn't going back until they changed the faces.
. . . He also believed it was a natural rock formation.

He didn't drive, but he kept putting nickels in the parking meters. He thought when you put enough money in that they gave you a car.

This guy was so dumb that if his mind suddenly went blank, it was an improvement.

The proudest day of his life was when he learned how to tie his own shoes. Then he broke his nose. Unfortunately, he'd tied them together.

He says he always has headaches because his hats are too big. Finally someone told him to try using a chin strap instead of a staple gun.

TOWN DRUNK

My uncle was the town drunk . . . and we lived in Chicago.
—*George Gobel*

A drunk walked up to a parking meter and put in a dime. The dial went to 60. He said, "How do you like that? I weigh an hour."—*Henny Youngman*

My father was never home; he was always drinking booze. He saw a sign saying "Drink Canada Dry." So he went up there.—*Henny Youngman*

I only drink to steady my nerves. Last night I got so steady that I couldn't move. —*Joe E. Lewis*

My grandfather drank a quart a day and he lived to be 103. I went to his cremation; that fire never did go out.—*Slappy White*

How can I tell when I've had enough to drink? Easy
—when my knees start to bend backwards.—*W. C. Fields*

. . .

Our town had a great town drunk. They built a monument to our town drunk. It's a beautiful bronze statue that's lying in the park.

Our town drunk didn't like to shave. He thought it was a terrible waste of shaving lotion.

This guy would drink anything. He's the only guy who even coated his body with suntan lotion . . . on the inside.

He really would drink anything. He was single-handedly responsible for our town's hair tonic blight of '63.

This guy saw double for all his adult life. He thought the entire town was made up of twins.
. . . He kept wondering where his went.

He was not only the town drunk; he was also the town War Memorial. We couldn't afford an eternal flame, so we just set fire to his breath.
. . . And he did his community service. They used to use his breath to kill all the weeds in Town Square.
. . . In the winter, he'd breathe on the interstate highway to melt the snow.
. . . Some good townspeople tried to rehabilitate him, and they did pretty well. For awhile there, they had him standing on his own two knees.

NEAT NEIGHBORS

It's easier to love humanity as a whole than to love one's neighbor.
—*Eric Hoffer*

Have I got a neat neighbor! She's so neat that she puts paper under the cuckoo clock.—*Henny Youngman*

My next-door neighbor is so neat that when her husband gets up at three in the morning to go to the bathroom, he returns and finds that the bed has been made.—*Milton Berle*

. . .

I live next door to the neatest housekeeper in the world. If she knew then that humans came from dirt, she would have refused to be born.

This lady is so neat that when you ring her doorbell, it sprays you with DDT.

This lady is a cleanliness fanatic. Her welcome mat is filled with Lysol.

This lady keeps her house so clean that dust has to request permission to land.

GROUCHY NEIGHBORS

This neighbor is a real grouch. If she were an island, she'd fight with the water. —*Bob Hope*

Our new neighbor is so grouchy! He moved into the neighborhood the other day and was fired on by the Welcome Wagon.—*Milton Berle*

I have a neighbor who is a total grouch. We had a block party once— we held it on another street.

Our town had the most grouchy neighbor in the world. In front of her door she had a man-eating welcome mat.

This lady was a real grouch. She had the personality of World War II.

This lady was so grouchy that when she came out to pick up her milk in the morning, it would curdle.

Nobody liked her. Even the paperboy wouldn't go near her house. He'd call her on the phone and read the news to her.

She was such a mean old lady that the local dentist would charge her extra. Apparently, fangs are a lot more difficult to work on.

She was so mean that she didn't like anything that was fun. The dentist even found out she was allergic to laughing gas.
. . . He had to give her snarling gas.

This lady was always frowning. Anytime she wanted to smile, she had to get two friends to help her.

She was mean. When she chased kids away from her house, everyone ran. Even the snails left skid marks.

Even the ASPCA had an injunction against her. She was scaring all the pit bulls in the neighborhood.

When the Welcome Wagon came to her door, she shot at it.

This lady was so bad that her dog put up a sign on her lawn that said, "Beware of My Master."

TOUGH NEIGHBORHOOD

I came from a tough neighborhood. Any cat with a tail was a tourist.
—*Milton Berle*

Our village idiot locked his keys in the car. It took him an hour and a half to get his wife out.

—*Henny Youngman*

I live in a rough neighborhood. We just put up a sign. It says, "Drive Fast. The life you save may be your own."—*Rodney Dangerfield*

I'll give you an idea how crime-ridden our neighborhood is. The other day I saw half a cop.—*Milton Berle*

Talk about tough neighborhoods. Where I lived nobody asked you the time, they just took your watch.—*Milton Berle*

Where I live, we don't worry about crime in the streets. They make house calls. —*Milton Berle*

Our neighborhood was so tough any kid with all his teeth was a sissy.

Guys in our neighborhood were so tough they used to steal hubcaps from cars . . . while they were moving.

The first words that babies would speak in our neighborhood were "Mama" and "Duck!"

I went to a very tough school. Every one of my classmates was the school bully.

Anytime I came home from school without a bloody nose, my mother knew I played hooky.

I got beat up so much in high school that I went to a four-year college just to heal.

We had so many fights in our school that recess was when we were all sent to a neutral corner.

At our school, the queen of the senior prom was selected by an arm-wrestling competition.

All the pictures in our yearbook were shown front and profile.

Our senior prom didn't need any chaperons. We had enough parole officers to keep order.

Over half the kids in our school graduated on a plea bargain.

On Valentine's Day, we exchanged heart-shaped Wanted posters of each other.

KING OF
THE ROAD

Automobiles

Driver's License

Bad Drivers

Traffic

Traffic Tickets

AUTOMOBILES

I'm having awful car troubles. The car won't start, and the payments won't stop.—*Milton Berle*

Boy, our new car is a real lemon! The windshield wipers are on the inside. The only time they do any good is when you're backing through a snowstorm with the rear window open.—*Phyllis Diller*

When I'm on the highway in my car, just once I'd like to see someone pass me without pointing to my tires.—*Rodney Dangerfield*

My new car is so modern you press a button and *it* presses a button. —*Henny Youngman*

I drove my car up to a toll bridge. The man said, "Fifty cents." I said, "Sold."—*Slappy White*

They have cars now that talk to you. I don't want a car that talks. When I get stopped by a highway patrolman, I don't want a car that could squeal on me.

Today's cars are aerodynamically designed. Yes, sir, they're built to sit in traffic jams at high speed.

I must admit I'm very dumb about buying used cars. I kick the doors and slam the tires.

I had a car once that was a real lemon. On this car even the ashtrays didn't work.

Talk about lemons! Most cars have a spare tire in the trunk; this car had a tow truck.

I bought one car that was a real mistake. The first time I parked it on the street, a cop gave me a ticket for littering.

I had a car once that was such a lemon that when I'd pull into a service station, I'd get a tank of gas and a six-pack of motor oil.

I had one automobile that was built so badly, it didn't come with a warranty—it came with an apology.

Our new car was such a lemon that the only thing we got with it that still works is the coupon book.

I bought one used car that was such a lemon, when I drove it home, the car got home a half hour before the motor did.

I bought a car once that I knew was going to be a lot of trouble because it was delivered by parcel post.
. . . It took me three days to get the stamps off the windshield.
. . . And the spare tire came with nine cents' postage due.

Who would give me a driver's license? I got two tickets on my written test. —*Phyllis Diller*

I sometimes have trouble starting my car. The ignition keeps spitting out the key.—*Phyllis Diller*

I bought my wife a new car. Three weeks ago she learned how to drive it. Last week she learned how to aim it.—*Henny Youngman*

To my wife, double parking means on top of another car. —*Dave Barry*

· · ·

This guy drove so fast that his driver's license was issued by the FAA. . . . He graduated from the Evel Knievel School of Driving.

I got my driver's license by default. They never found the officer who gave me my test.

I'm such a bad driver that I had three accidents just taking the written driver's test.

I've never been a very good driver. I got four traffic tickets on my written test.. . . and two more during the eye exam.

I refused to take the eye exam at my driver's test. I figured: why should 1? I never look where I'm going anyway.

An officer said to me once, "Do you know it's against the law to drive with-out a license?" I said, "Then arrest the traffic judge. He's the one who took it away from me."

BAD DRIVERS

One day my wife drove up the side of a building . . . and hit another woman driving down.—*Milton Berle*

Whenever I rent a car, in order to cut down on the mileage rate, I back up everywhere.—*Woody Allen*

A wife told her husband, "Be an angel and let me drive." He did and he is.—*Milton Berle*

My wife doesn't stop for red lights anymore. She says,
"If you've seen one or two, you've seen them all."—*Dave Barry*

Never lend your car to anyone to whom you have given birth.
—*Erma Bombeck*

My wife called me. She said, "There's water in the carburetor." I said, "Where's the car? " She said, "In the lake."—*Henny Youngman*

The best way to stop the noise in the car is to let her drive.—*Milton Berle*

Fang is a typical husband. When I drive, he complains about every telephone pole I hit. But does he ever compliment me on the ones I miss?
—*Phyllis Diller*

. . .

My wife is such a bad driver that when she goes into the garage, the car puts its tail pipe between its legs.

When my wife drives, the little statue climbs off the dashboard and crawls into the glove compartment.

One day I came home complaining about the car. I said, "Do you know that's the third clutch I've had to replace?" My wife said, "Don't blame me. I never use it."

My uncle is a maniac on the freeways. He only gets about six miles to the cuss word.. . . The other day my uncle honked at twelve cars, shook his fist at seven, made obscene gestures at four, and cursed three—and he hadn't pulled out of the driveway yet.

The way people drive today, half of them should be pulled over by police, and the other half should be pulled over by their psychiatrists.

Driving changes people. Everybody on the road today is a regular Dr. Jekyll and Mr. Goodwrench.

I've actually seen drivers roll down their windows and curse passing motorists—from cars that were being towed.

Years ago you had to roll down your window to curse a passing motorist; nowadays you can call him on your car phone.

I saw a guy drive right through a red light the other day, and the guy behind him got angry because he didn't drive through it fast enough.

Some people treat driving as a means of transportation. Others consider it a contact sport.

It may be the fault of the car manufacturers. Too many drivers take the term *bumpers* literally.

Driving today is America's last surviving form of guerrilla warfare.

The way some people drive, it seems they should put on war paint before turning on the ignition.

Many people drive simply to get where they're going; others, for revenge.

We should have stayed with horseback as the predominant means of transportation. At least with horses we didn't have to put up with obnoxious bumper stickers.

It seems today that road courtesy went out with running boards.

We all hate aggressive drivers. They're the ones who try to get back at us after we cut them off.

I know one driver who gets on the road and immediately pulls into the fast lane . . . whether there's another car there already or not.

The way some people drive, the car is not considered an automobile. It's considered an accomplice.

I have one friend who speeds constantly. His one goal in life is to never have another car in front of him.

You know you're getting too angry behind the wheel when you can light up without using the car's cigarette lighter.

TRAFFIC

Traffic was so heavy that it was bumper-to-bumper. A man pushed in his cigarette lighter, and the man in the car in front said, "Ouch!"
—*Henny Youngman*

The only way to solve the traffic problem is to pass a law that only paid-for cars are allowed to use the highways.—*Will Rogers*

The traffic is so heavy in New York's Midtown that one day I saw three cars chasing the same pedestrian.—*Jan Murray*

. . .

Traffic was so bad on the freeway the other day that on the way home I had to stop three times to make car payments.

The roads are getting packed nowadays. The only way you can change lanes now is to buy the car next to you.

Traffic used to be bumper-to-bumper; now it's worse. It's windshield-to-windshield.

It used to take three hours by horse-drawn buggy to go from one end of the city to the other. Today it takes you that long just to get on the freeway.

People don't want to be in traffic that much. It's just that there's no place else to go when you can't find a parking place.

The law says there should be five car lengths between you and the car in front of you. In order to get that you have to talk at least four people into staying home.

Traffic is getting so bad nowadays that you can change a flat tire without losing your place in line.

I remember how embarrassed people used to get when their car stalled on the highway. Nowadays, it's no problem; you just blend in with the normal traffic flow.

The only way to get home on time in today's traffic is to take the day off.

Traffic is so congested that a pedestrian nowadays is someone in a hurry.

Cars are jammed so close together that they may soon sell gas with deodorant in it.

I watched the young couple in front of me "necking" all the way home on the freeway. They were in separate cars.

Traffic is so bad nowadays that even people who are going to stay home have to leave early.

Traffic is so congested today. If you throw a hubcap during rush hour, it'll probably get to work before you do.

There's no courtesy on the highways today. One man put his arm out the window to signal a lane change and somebody stole his watch.

Traffic is really congested on our highways. One Cadillac pulled over to the side of the road, opened its hood, and two Volkswagens drove out.

TRAFFIC
TICKETS

I got a jaywalking ticket, which is the dumbest ticket of all. I said, "Is this going to go on my record, or can I go to Walking School and have this taken off?"—*Gary Shandling*

I went to court for a parking ticket. I pleaded insanity.—*Steven Wright*

You know it's time to go on a diet when you're standing next to your car and get a ticket for double parking.—*Totie Fields*

In my glove compartment, I had ten moving-violation citations, which are like savings bonds—the longer you keep them, the more they mature.
—*Bill Cosby*

I get so many tickets so fast that I had to replace my glove compartment with a filing cabinet.

I've got a master's degree from Traffic School.

This one town was a real speed trap. I once got a ticket for speeding while I was fixing a flat.
. . . Another policeman there gave me a ticket for having my windshield wipers going the wrong way on a one-way street.

A cop gave me a ticket for going the wrong way on a one-way street. I said, "You know, you'll make a lot more money if you let me go and ticket everybody else."

A policeman stopped me and said, "Let me see your driver's license." I said, "Officer, you've seen how I drive. Do you think anybody would give me a license?"

A policeman stopped me and said, "You know, this car has been reported stolen." I said, "Well, I've found it. Is there a reward?"

A cop gave me tickets for speeding, reckless driving, going through a traffic signal, and driving without a license. About the only thing I did right was that I was sitting on the correct side of the vehicle.

I'm such an optimist. Every time a policeman drives alongside and asks me to pull over, I think he wants to ask for directions.

A police car trailed me for 10 miles and finally pulled me over for speeding. He said, "OK, where's the fire?" I said, "I don't know, officer, but you and I are going to be the first ones there."

I'll never forget the first ticket I ever got—$30 for passing on the wrong side of a subway train.

I WONDER WHERE MY LUGGAGE WENT

Travel

Airlines

Hotels

Restaurants

Near & Far

TRAVEL

"If you look like your passport photo, you're too ill to travel."
—*Will Kommen*

Travel is very educational. I can now say "Kaopectate" in seven different languages—*Bob Hope*

Actually, I'm an advocate of separate vacations—the children's and ours.
—*Erma Bombeck*

They spell it "V–I–N–C–I" and pronounce it "Vinchy." Foreigners always spell better than they pronounce.—*Mark Twain*

I traveled to China. Boy, there ought to be a law against making an ocean that wide. —*Will Rogers*

She was so ugly that Customs wouldn't let her enter the country without a crate .—*Milton Berle*

. . .

He used to do so much traveling that he never needed a plane. He had a business suit made with a fuel tank added.

He flies around the world so much that at his last physical they found traces of feathers.

He travels so much that he has to wait till the morning paper comes to find out what city he's in.

He's done so much traveling that every time he sits down, he puts his seat back and his tray table in its upright and locked position.

I have jet lag. That's when you arrive and your luggage is in better shape than you are.

Jet lag is nature's way of making you look like your passport photo.

I travel a lot. I go to about half as many places as my luggage does.

I checked my luggage last week. The guy tore off the stubs and said, "Here are your lottery tickets."

 *AIRLINES*

If the Lord had wanted people to fly, He would have made it simpler for people to get to the airport.—*Milton Berle*

I don't fly on account of my religion—I'm a devout coward.
—*Henny Youngman*

I was on an airplane. The pilot came running down the aisle with a parachute strapped to his back. He said, "Don't be alarmed, but we're having a little trouble with the landing gear. I'm gonna run on ahead and warn them at the airport."—*Slappy White*

With today's technology, flying is much faster. To give you an idea of how fast we traveled: When we left we had two rabbits, and when we got there, we still had only two.—*Bob Hope*

The Concorde travels at twice the speed of sound, which is fun, except that you can't hear the movie until two hours after you land.
—*Howie Mandel*

I flew over here on the Concorde. That plane is so fast that it gives you an extra couple of hours to look for your luggage.—*Bob Hope*

Flying is so expensive these days. I took an economy flight. There wasn't any movie, but they flew low over the drive-ins.—*Red Buttons*

. . .

People are afraid of airplanes. I got in the ticket line behind an honest man once. He said to the clerk, "Give me two chances to Pittsburgh."

I don't worry about flying. I figure there can't be anything on the plane more dangerous than the airline food.

If it weren't for airlines, we'd be up to our necks in honey-roasted peanuts.

Flying is getting very expensive nowadays. The other day I saw a bird riding a bicycle.

All domestic air flights are nonsmoking now. The most fun smokers can have on airplanes now is turning down the food.

The only way you can smoke on a domestic flight nowadays is to be one of the engines.

Some smokers are trying to get around the regulation by disguising themselves as luggage.
. . . They figure it's worth the risk of getting lost.

If you're on a long flight and you absolutely have to smoke, you can always step outside.

. . . It's a long first step, but for some smokers it's worth it.

I was on an airline that was so cheap that when they rolled those little steps away, the plane fell over on its side.

I was on an airline that was so cheap that we had to fly at a low altitude. The captain explained that if we flew any higher, the sun would melt the wax wings.

This airline was so cheap that instead of a movie, they put on a high-school play.

 # HOTELS

What a hotel! The towels were so big and fluffy, you could hardly close your suitcase.—*Henny Youngman*

There was only one hotel in my hometown. It wasn't much, but at least it had a bridal suite. It was the room with the lock on the door.
—*Herb Shriner*

My hotel room was so small, every time I put the key in the lock, I broke the window.—*Milton Berle*

My hotel room was so small, I couldn't brush my teeth sideways.
—*Milton Berle*

I once had a hotel room that was so small that it had removable door-knobs—just in case you wanted to bend over.—*Fred Allen*

Hotels are getting bigger and bigger. I called for room service at one of them, and my meal arrived by UPS.

Some of the hotels are too big. It's annoying to have to carry your passport every time you want to go down to the lobby.

I went to one hotel and just wanted to stay overnight. They wouldn't let me. They said that wouldn't give me enough time to get to my room.

This is a very big hotel. They give two weather reports here—one for inside the hotel and one for outside.

This is really an immense building. I don't know whether this hotel has a manager or a governor.

This hotel is so big, I went up to the desk and said, "Do I ask for a reservation or apply for citizenship?"

This is a giant hotel. Room service is a long-distance call.

This hotel is really immense. It's the only one I've ever seen where the bellhops are on horseback.

This hotel is so large that before they carry your luggage to your room, they ask if there are any perishables in them.

I stayed in one hotel that was so chintzy that I had to carry my own bags up to my room. I wouldn't have minded if I were a bigger tipper.

Nobody at this hotel had any self-confidence. The guy who operated the elevator had to stop three times to ask directions.

This hotel was very cheap, but they still have a change of linen every day. Room 301 changes with Room 303, Room 302 changes with Room 304 ...

RESTAURANTS NEAR&FAR

Last night I ordered an entire meal in French, and even the waiter was surprised. I was in a Chinese restaurant.—*Henny Youngman*

My split personality is getting worse. Yesterday I ate in a restaurant alone and asked for two checks.—*Rodney Dangerfield*

I once crossed a waiter with a tiger. I don't know what I got, but I tip him big .—*Milton Berle*

Fang took me to a restaurant that he said was secluded. That means the Board of Health can't find it.—*Phyllis Diller*

I was arrested today for scalping low numbers at the deli.—*Steven Wright*

I've been trying to get my husband to take me out to dinner for so long, that when he finally said yes, I couldn't eat.—*Phyllis Diller*

A holdup man walks into a Chinese restaurant, and he says, "Give me all your money." The man says, "To go?"—*Slappy White*

I was in a restaurant. I called the waitress over and said, "This coffee isn't fit for a pig." She said, "Oh, I'll take it away and bring you some that is."—*Milton Berle*

. . .

My wife says the nicest thing about eating out is that no matter what you order someone else is going to have to do the dishes.

When we were getting ready to go out and eat, my wife said, "I feel like a hamburger tonight." And she must have, because she put on secret sauce instead of lipstick.

My wife said, "Get your elbows off the table." So, I did and my face fell in the soup.

We went to a very expensive restaurant the other night. When you come in, they let you keep your hat and coat, but you have to check your wallet.

This restaurant charged exorbitant prices. I asked the waiter, "What's the catch of the day?" He said, "You are."

The portions at this restaurant were so small that I had to fill up on parsley.

I went to one restaurant and ordered Tuna Surprise. The surprise was that the tuna fish was tainted.

The waiter at one restaurant advised me that they were no longer offering the special of the day. It had exploded.

Never eat at a restaurant where the place mats have instructions for the Heimlich maneuver printed on them.

Never eat at a restaurant where menu items are marked with an asterisk, signifying those items covered by the restaurant's insurance policy.

This restaurant was so bad I asked the waiter, "What do you recommend?" He said, "Get out while you still can."

Never eat at a restaurant that lists Pepto-Bismol soufflé as a dessert.

I said to my waiter, "What would you recommend?" He said, "The restaurant down the street."

I asked the waiter what was in the Veal Caribbean. He said, "I don't know, and considering the condition of the chef, he probably doesn't know either."

What a dump this restaurant was. Flyswatters were an item on the menu.

This restaurant was so cheap and so lousy, they gave us the check faceup and turned the food over.

The food at this restaurant was so bad that in the kitchen the flies threw themselves at the flypaper.
. . . It was safer than landing on the special of the day.
This restaurant was so bad that I not only had a fly in my soup, but the entire pair of trousers.

This restaurant was so bad that its doggie bags were marked "not for consumption by real dogs."

The food here was bad. I said to the waiter, "There's a fly in my soup." He said, "Let's hope for his sake he doesn't swallow any."

I went to a Middle Eastern restaurant where I knew they served camel meat. I asked the waiter for a glass of water, and they didn't bring it for 10 days.
. . . I ordered a hamburger and the waiter asked, "One hump or two?"

This restaurant knew their food was bad. As we left, the maitre d' said, "Please come back and see us when you've recovered."

OUR WORLD & WELCOME TO IT

Weather

Drought

Earthquakes

Water

Pollution

Air Pollution

Spring

Summer

Fall

Winter

 **WEATHER**

Let's face it, our world is the best place to live on Earth. —*Gene Perret*

It's been so cold this winter, the Golden Girls had to be pump-started.
—*Bob Hope*

It was so cold I saw a politician with his hands in his own pockets.
—*Henny Youngman*

It was so cold I saw a polar bear wearing a grizzly.—*Milton Berle*

The coldest winter I ever spent was a summer in San Francisco.
—*Mark Twain*

It was so hot out today, I saw a Dalmatian with his spots on the ground.
—*Pat McCormick*

. . .

If you want to get an idea of how hot it is, try cleaning your oven the next
time from the inside.
. . . while you're roasting a turkey.

It's so hot that the grapes in the Fruit-of-the-Loom label turned to raisins.

It's really been hot. I saw a dog chasing a cat in Beverly Hills the other
day, and it was so hot that both of their chauffeurs passed out.

This heat is tough on everybody. I saw a flock of birds heading north today, and they were hitchhiking.

. . . And they would only accept rides in air-conditioned cars.

Soon we're going to have four seasons—summer, simmer, broil, and bake.

It was really hot today. At the Hollywood Wax Museum, John Wayne melted down to the size of Mickey Rooney.

It was really hot today. In fact, one poor dog had his tongue out so far his tail disappeared.

It's been pretty cold lately. The other day I saw a dog chasing a cat, and they were both ice skating.

It was so cold that everything was freezing. Cows were giving cream by the scoop.

It was so cold in New York that the Statue of Liberty was holding the torch *under* her dress.

Last night, it was so cold I fell out of bed and cracked my pajamas.

In cold weather like this, you're constantly numb. If you sat on a tack, you wouldn't notice it until the spring thaw.

It's so cold around here that everything is frozen. I had to wear a bullet-proof vest to take a shower.

It was so cold last week that my grandpa's teeth were chattering—and they were home on the dresser.

I have a real good electric blanket that's specially made for this cold weather. It has three settings: WARM, WARMER, and THE LIFE YOU SAVE MAY BE YOUR OWN.
. . . It has a fourth setting, too. But if you put it on that, you need a pardon from the Governor to turn it off.

It was so cold that we circled the airport six times. It took that long for the plane to get the courage to set its tail down on the frozen runway.

Everything in the country was covered with snow. I was sure glad when our plane rolled to a stop in New York—especially since we had landed in Chicago.

It's been so cold lately that people have to use an ice pick to get comfortable on their water beds.

It's been so cold lately; the Abominable Snowman moved to Palm Springs.

People are trying everything to keep warm. General Electric has even come out with a new Crock-Pot that sleeps two.

This cold weather is really something. The bathroom in my hotel room was equipped with hot and cold running ice cubes.

On Groundhog Day, if the groundhog comes out of his hole and sees his shadow, it means six more weeks of winter. It's been so cold this year that he came out of his hole and bought a condominium in Florida.

It's been so cold lately that it's costing doctors a lot of money. They have to hire four assistants to get people to strip to the waist.

 # DROUGHT

There's such a drought that some restaurants are charging for water. There was a big argument in Beverly Hills the other day. One customer was angry because they brought him the wrong year.

This is the worst drought in history. I saw a woman in the supermarket yesterday buying bottled dust.

This drought is so bad that at most of the prisons, they're serving the prisoners bread and bread.

Water is so scarce right now that I read where two fish just bought themselves a mobile home.

The scarcity of water is causing real problems. Last week our porch caught fire and the firemen had to blow it out.

The government says we're not allowed to water our lawns. Yesterday four earthworms came to my door and asked to borrow a cup of water.

The drought is real bad. I turned on my faucet the other day and an I.O.U. came out.

EARTH-QUAKES

Those earthquakes in California are something. It's frightening when your bedroom gets up and goes down to breakfast before you do.—*Bob Hope*

My family and I have come up with a course of action for an earthquake. At the first tremor, we get out of bed calmly, stand in a doorway, and start screaming. Maybe you know our system under another name: panic. —*Milton Berle*

I don't know if that was a strong quake, but my zip code changed three times.—*Milton Berle*

We have a lot of quakes in California. Half of the time you don't even have to stir your own coffee in the morning. Mother Nature does it for you.

One Los Angeles television station offered an "Earthquake Survival Guide." I sent in a self-addressed stamped envelope, and they sent me a map to Kansas.

One guy was getting a tattoo when an earthquake hit. He now has his girlfriend's name written across his chest, around his back, and down his left leg.

There are a lot of earthquakes in southern California. You know those addresses they paint on the curb in front of your house? In southern California, they do them in pencil.

Experts say the way your animal behaves can sometimes help predict an earthquake. The night before the last earthquake hit, my poodle packed a suitcase and headed back to France.

286

After the earthquake, my house is still up on the hill, but my view just got lowered.

—*Bob Hope*

WATER POLLUTION

All the drinks in Hawaii have something floating in them. It's kind of like our water back in Los Angeles.—*Bob Hope*

. . .

Our waters are polluted. Last week a half-dozen saltwater fish came to my house and asked to use the pool.

The water is so polluted that not too many people fish anymore. One guy did. He caught a sea bass wearing a gas mask.

There's so much oil in our waters nowadays that you can catch two kinds of tuna—regular or unleaded.

In California they have No Smoking signs on the beach. There's so much oil in the water that the ocean could catch fire.

Last week a whale washed up on the beach. He claimed he slipped out of the water.

In California, people wipe their feet when they come out of the ocean.

All of our waters are filthy. Recently someone reported that they discovered water under Lake Erie.

AIR POLLUTION

There's so much pollution in the air now that if it weren't for our lungs, there'd be no place to put it all.—*Robert Orben*

Fight air pollution—inhale.—*Red Buttons*

I don't like all this fresh air. I'm from Los Angeles. I don't trust any air I can't see.—*Bob Hope*

The smog was so bad that I opened my mouth to yawn and chipped a tooth!—*Bob Hope*

. . .

Nowadays, you get up in the morning, open the window, take a deep breath, and you're in no condition to do your exercises.

People nowadays wake up and go outside to have a bite of fresh air.

But it's still a thrill to spot the first robin of spring—
having a coughing fit on your lawn.

People on this Earth say God is dead. I don't think so. I think He's just staying in heaven for reasons of His health.

I had a friend who went to the doctor to have his heart checked. The doctor put the stethoscope on his chest and said, "Take a deep breath." His heart was fine; the deep breath killed him.

New York is working very hard to clear up air pollution. They want to have nothing but healthy people being mugged in Central Park.

The politicians are getting active in environmental safety. From our air, they want to remove smog, auto emissions, toxic chemicals, and acid rain. If they take all that out of the air, what's going to hold the birds up?

I do wish they would eliminate acid rain. I'm getting tired of lugging around that lead umbrella.

Air pollution is commonplace nowadays. Everyone's eyes water so much that they're selling contact lenses that come with windshield wipers.

SPRING

Spring showers in California bring mud slides. That's when you look out the window of your car and find out that your house is making better time than you are.—*Bob Hope*

Spring is when the birds return from their trip south for the winter, and they're all grumpy about having to return from their vacation.

. . .

Birds who migrate are lucky. At least they don't have to make the trip with the kids screaming in the back of the car.

Some birds don't go south for the winter. I suppose, like the rest of us, they can't afford it.

Spring is when a young man's fancy lightly turns to thoughts of love. For most young men, so are summer, fall, and winter.

You can almost smell the romance in the air in spring. It's either that or all those scratch-and-sniff ads in the magazines.

Spring is such a gorgeous season because the earth turns green. It blends so beautifully with the brown of our skies.

290

Spring is a time when the umpire shouts, "Play ball!" and the Dodgers shout back, "We're trying, we're trying! . . ."

Spring is when Mother Nature awakens from her long winter's sleep. Thank goodness she's in a better mood when she wakes up than I am. . . . Otherwise, spring would be hell on Earth until she's had her second cup of coffee.

If you had to pick a color to symbolize spring it would be green, because it's in spring that taxes are due.

In California, spring is when the swallows return to Capistrano. In the Midwest, it's when feeling returns to your feet.

Spring is a nice time of year. It's when *damn* and *snow* become two separate words again.

Spring, they say, is when a young man's fancy turns to thoughts of love. . . . But I wonder how anyone can think of love with a turned fancy? . . . I turned my ankle once and couldn't think of anything but getting to a doctor.

Spring is a happy time of life—especially for baseball players. That's when they start collecting their million-dollar salaries.

All the birds begin to return in spring, which means you probably have to get your car washed more often.

All the birds return in spring, which is great unless you happen to be a worm. . . . especially one who gets up early.

Spring is a time of year when the birds and the bees become active again. From what my father told me about them, they should all be in jail.

Spring is the time of year when everything turns green—especially the cheese you've had in your refrigerator since last summer.

Spring is when everything turns green . . . including my father, who knows that income tax time is near.

SUMMER

It was so hot the other day, I passed Grant's tomb and the window was open.—*Milton Berle*

. . .

Summer is vacation time. That's when you go away for two weeks and your money goes away forever.

Everyone should take a summer vacation. Remember, mosquitoes have to eat, too.

I love summer vacation. It's so relaxing . . . to get back to work again.

I found out what I don't like about family vacations—family.

My wife wanted to go to Hawaii for our vacation; I wanted to go to Bermuda. So we split the difference. We stayed home.

The heat this summer has been terrible. I took off the clothes I wore yesterday and threw them in the hamper. It threw them back out.

It was so hot today that now I think I have a genuine feel for how Frosty the Snowman feels at the end of the song.

It was so hot in Arizona even the cactuses were checking into hotels for the weekend.

It's been so hot lately that they had to put sandbags around the Hollywood Wax Museum. If Roseanne Barr melts, she could wipe out Sunset Boulevard.

It was so hot in Palm Springs that even the lizards were wearing Bermuda shorts.

It's been hot lately. I've got underarm stains on clothes I haven't even taken out of the closet yet.

FALL

Fall is my favorite season in Los Angeles, watching the birds change color and fall from the trees.—*David Letterman*

It's nice to work in New York City in the fall. It's nice to walk down Madison Avenue and see the trees turning from charcoal gray to charcoal brown.—*Joe E. Lewis*

. . .

Every year in fall many things in nature turn to pretty orange, yellow, red, and brown. I have things in my refrigerator that do that every month.

Fall is a time of glorious color. It's the season when Mother Nature thinks she's Ted Turner.

If Mother Nature wanted autumn to be really beautiful, she would have raked up the leaves herself.

My wife loves it when the leaves turn all different colors. Yet she got very upset when the ring I bought her did the same thing.

In the fall the leaves turn different colors and get immortalized by poets. When your teeth do that, you get a lecture from your dentist.

Autumn is when the leaves turn and fall. I have an uncle who does that every time he tries to leave the corner bar.

Every autumn I watch the first leaf fall from the tree. I watch it float gracefully downward and land softly on the earth. I turn and hear my wife say, "Don't you think it's about time you raked the lawn?"

Fall is when the leaves on the trees know their usefulness is done and they depart gracefully. Politicians should be made to watch and learn.

In fall the trees go from having plenty of leaves to having none at all. For us humans, that happens at tax time.

The autumn leaves turn deep brown and get dry and brittle. It reminds me a lot of my cooking.

In autumn all of nature turns glorious, brilliant, vibrant colors. You can get the same effect stubbing your toe in a dark bedroom.

In fall all of nature keeps turning different and unusual colors. It reminds me of a cheap watchband I once bought.. . . It didn't last through the winter, either.

My wife is always after me to rake up the leaves. I'm always saying, "Wait a few months; the snow will cover them."

I hate raking leaves. It would be a lot easier if the birds would stay here, and the trees on my lawn would go south for the winter.

Fall is a time when nature turns many different shades and then loses everything. You and I do the same thing when we get seasick.

The trees lose all of their leaves in the fall. It's strange. They're the only things that get undressed for winter.

In autumn the leaves turn different colors and begin to fall. I have an Uncle George who does that every Friday evening.

I think nature is very inconsiderate in fall. I can understand the trees' losing their foliage. I went bald several years ago, but I didn't leave my hair lying all over someone's lawn.

WINTER

I don't want to find fault, but I wonder if God ever considered having snow fall up?—*Robert Orben*

A lot of people like snow. I find it an unnecessary freezing of water. —*Carl Reiner*

It's so cold here that a pin-up calendar isn't a luxury, it's a necessity. —*Bob Hope*

This town only had two seasons—winter and "Road Under Repair." —*George Gobel*

It was so cold that even politicians were walking around with their hands in their own pockets.—*Bob Hope*

LIFE & ITS AFTER EFFECTS

Birth

Old Age

Death

Spiritual Matters

Heaven

Hell

Reincarnation

BIRTH

I was so ugly that when I was born, the doctor slapped my mother.
—*Henny Youngman*

I ran into an old friend from the town where I was born. "Red," he exclaimed, "You sure have put on a lot of weight." "Yeah, I only weighed seven pounds when I was born."—*Red Skelton*

Once my husband said to me, "I'm going to have some coffee. Do you want me to put some hot water on for you?" I thought that was the least he could do, considering I was giving birth.—*Phyllis Diller*

When I was born, I was so surprised I couldn't talk for a year and a half.—*Gracie Allen*

I was born modest; not all over, but in spots.—*Mark Twain*

I was born in Philadelphia. I wanted to be near my mother.

My birth must have come as quite a surprise. I didn't even have a chance to dress for it.

. . .

I don't know why I was born in a hospital. Up until then I was never sick a day in my life.

I don't remember much about my birth. I was only a child at the time.

I weighed six pounds, eight ounces when I was born. I eat more than that now for lunch.

After I was born, the doctor sent my father a bill for $500. I don't know why—Mom and I did all the work.

My father was so happy when I was born he rushed out to tell all his friends. We expect him back any day now.

My Dad said I was the cutest baby he'd ever seen except that I had no nose. Then he discovered he was holding me upside down and backwards.

 **OLD AGE**

I've been around for awhile. When I was a boy, the Dead Sea was only sick. —*George Burns*

You know you're old when everything hurts, and what doesn't hurt, doesn't work.—*George Burns*

With today's technology, they have artificial replacements for everything. You don't have to worry about getting old; you have to worry about rusting.—*George Burns*

Old age is when your liver spots show through your gloves. —*Phyllis Diller*

One nice thing about old age—you can whistle while you brush your teeth. —*Jack Carter*

. . .

I have Old-Timers' Disease. I don't forget things; I lose interest in them.

I think people should enjoy old age. It's the one thing they can do better than the youngsters.

I'm going through my second childhood right now. It's my fourth trip through.

My uncle has had every part of his body replaced. He's still alive, but hardly anybody recognizes him.

Remember, you're as young as you feel. If you don't feel anything, you're old.

I suppose I'm getting up in years. If I were a bottle of wine I'd be worth a fortune now.

Age is only a state of mind—that is, provided you have one left.

After a certain age, the only things you're allowed to do are things you either don't want to do or have already forgotten how
to do.

I know a fellow who is so old that he has one of the few Social Security cards left with the number written in Roman numerals.

He has hit that time of life when, if you blow out all the candles on your cake, you not only get your wish, but you also get a hernia.

I was always taught to respect my elders. But it's getting harder and harder—to find one.

You know you're getting on in years when your life
flashes before your eyes, and you fall asleep during it.

Older Americans are really in good shape. We used to offer our seats to
old ladies on a bus. Now they're in good enough shape to *take* them.

They are really keeping young. Yesterday I saw four old ladies helping a
Boy Scout across the street.
. . . It took four of them because he didn't want to go.

It's nice that we got our older citizens out of rocking chairs and wheel-
chairs. Now they're starting to hang out in groups on street corners.

DEATH

MAN: Do you realize that every time I draw a mortal breath an immortal
soul passes on into eternity?
MARK TWAIN: Ever try cloves?—*Mark Twain*

Dying is not popular; it has never caught on. That's understandable; it's
bad for the complexion.—*George Burns*

This guy dies and leaves the shortest will. It says, "Being in my sound
mind, I spent my money."—*Henny Youngman*

We usually meet all our relatives only at funerals, where someone always
observes, "Too bad we can't get together more often."—*Sam Levenson*

I'm not afraid to die, I just don't want to be there when it happens.
—*Woody Allen*

Death is one way of putting an end to all that junk mail.

Death is a way of saying, "Yesterday was the last day of the rest of your life."

Death is nature's way of saying, "Hold all my calls."

Death is the last thing everybody does, and it's the first thing a lot of them do correctly.

Death is the ultimate in packing light for a trip.

Death is nature's way of missing the last exit before the toll booth.

SPIRITUAL MATTERS

God sneezed. What could I say to Him?—*Henny Youngman*

I believe our Heavenly Father invented man because He was disappointed in the monkey.—*Mark Twain*

If only God would give me a clear sign! Like making a large deposit in my name at a Swiss bank.—*Woody Allen*

Definition of a dead atheist: All dressed up and nowhere to go.—*Woody Woodbury*

The reason God made man before woman was because He didn't want any suggestions.—*Sam Levenson*

. . .

God knows all things. He'd be a great person to have to help you with your homework, wouldn't He?

I know God is up there even though I can't see Him. In Los Angeles, I know the sky is up there even though I can't see that either.

How can some people say God is dead? We're not even sure about Elvis.

I once prayed in a hotel, and they charged me a 75-cent long-distance service charge.

Sometimes technology can be a detriment. I tried to pray the other day and got God's answering machine.
. . . My preacher told me not to worry about it. If my prayer had been really important, they would have beeped Him.

Eternal rest sounds comforting in the pulpit. Well, you try it once and see how heavy time will hang on your hands.—*Mark Twain*

When asked to join a discussion of eternal life and future punishment, I replied, "I am silent of necessity; I have friends in both places."
—*Mark Twain*

You have to be really good to go to heaven. Years ago my parents told me the same thing about Disneyland.

Heaven is very important to my mom. She's always wanted to live in a gated community.

You have to die to go to heaven. It's kind of the ultimate retirement village.

I'm worried about going to heaven. When St. Peter opens up the Pearly Gates, what do you tip him?

Wouldn't it be terrible to get to heaven and see a sign posted on the Pearly Gates that reads: "This Property Protected by the Ajax Alarm System"?

Only good people go to heaven. So the *National Enquirer* up there makes for very dull reading.

What do you do if you want to go to heaven, but you hate harp music?

I have this fear that when I get to heaven, God's going to hand me a set of angel wings, and I'm going to have to tell Him I'm afraid of heights.

One guy got to heaven and became an angel. He said, "Now you give me the wings. I died in a bungee-jumping accident."

There is one bad feature of going to heaven—anything you bought on a lifetime guarantee is no longer covered.

Heaven is forever. So bring plenty of reading material.

HELL

I do benefits for all religions. I'd hate to go to hell on a technicality.
—*Bob Hope*

A diplomat is a person who can tell you to go to hell in such a way that you actually look forward to the trip.—*Caskie Stinnett*

My wife converted me to religion. I never believed in hell until I married her.—*Hal Roach*

People in hell—where do they tell people to go?—*Red Skelton*

. . .

It's possible that hell could just be heaven without room service.

Hell is forever; it just seems longer.

Hell is one place where losers can never say "Wait 'til next year."

Heaven is for good people. Hell is for those who don't want to spend eternity hanging around with good people.

I wonder if hell has smoking and nonsmoking sections.

Hell is a place full of fire and brimstone—kind of like Los Angeles during the dry season.

Wouldn't it be ironic if on the gates of hell there were a sign posted that read: "We Reserve the Right to Refuse Admittance to Anyone"?

I don't want to be sent to hell, but with the luck I've been having with my travel agent lately . . .

Hell is supposed to be a bad place, but you can't believe that because everyone who goes there is a liar.

REINCARNATION

I happen to be the suspicious type. For instance, I've always felt that reincarnation is just a sneaky way to sell more tombstones.—*Robert Orben*

If I believed in reincarnation, I'd come back as a sponge.—*Woody Allen*

I believe in reincarnation. I've had other lives, I know. I've had clues. First of all, I'm exhausted.—*Carol Siskind*

There's nothing wrong with you that reincarnation won't cure.
—*Jack E. Leonard*

In the next life, I'd like to come back as an oyster. Then I'd only have to be good from September to April. —*Gracie Allen*

Reincarnation may be nature's way of saying, "Okay, let's make it the best two out of three."

If I'm going to come back to life, why am I dieting so much to keep this one in shape?

I like the idea of reincarnation. Toys today are so much more fun than they were when I was a kid.

I don't know if I've ever lived before. I can't remember half the things I've done in this life.

I don't like the thought of reincarnation. It's discouraging to think that I may have lived ten or twelve lives before this, and I still don't know how to hit a golf ball.

If there is such a thing as reincarnation, then death isn't really death. It's just a chance to get a quick shower and a change of clothes.

Just on the outside chance that there is reincarnation, I'm leaving everything in my will to me—whoever I may be at the time.

I'll go along with reincarnation with one reservation: I don't want to come back in the next life at an entry-level position.

There could just be such a thing as reincarnation. So, don't make fun of your great-grandfather. He just might be you.

You die, you come back. You die, you come back. You die, you come back. It's a terrible way to go through eternity
. . . as a yo-yo.

HOLIDAYS & CELEBRATIONS

Halloween

Christmas

New Year's Eve

Birthdays

Anniversaries

Parties

HALLOWEEN

I went to a Halloween party dressed as the Equator. As people walked towards me they got warmer.—*Steven Wright*

I was so ugly as a kid, I had to trick-or-treat over the phone.
—*Rodney Dangerfield*

I was so ugly as a kid we never had a jack-'o-lantern. They just stuck me in the window.—*Rodney Dangerfield*

. . .

I always used to scare the neighbors on Halloween. I dressed up as my brother.

Halloween is an educational holiday. If it weren't for that day none of us would know what a goblin looked like.

I love Halloween. The Christmas decorations look so nice in the department stores.

Halloween is when people try to frighten you into giving them goodies. In some ways, it's a lot like government.

One of the worst feelings in the world is to show up at a costume party not wearing a costume— and no one notices.

I know one guy who was tall, slender, and bald. On Halloween he'd paint his head blue and go to the party as a ballpoint pen.

Women who are looking for Mr. Right enjoy Halloween. For that one night, at least, they can settle for Mr. "You-don't-look-half-bad-with-a-mask-on."

Halloween is not a big holiday at most nudist camps. It's hard to dress up where no clothes are allowed.
. . . Besides, even with a mask, people can usually tell who you are.

Halloween is when you're constantly threatened with "Trick or treat!" It has a lot in common with election night, doesn't it?

Halloween is a night when everyone tries to look grotesque, as opposed to the rest of the year when only rock stars do.

CHRISTMAS

Santa Claus has the right idea. Visit people once a year.—*Victor Borge*

This guy is so cheap; he sends one Christmas card out each year . . .
in the form of a chain letter.—*Phyllis Diller*

I gave my wife a brand new watch for Christmas—waterproof, shock-proof, unbreakable, and antimagnetic. Absolutely nothing could happen to it—she lost it.—*Milton Berle*

As my children got older, I got used to buying Christmas presents that (A)

I couldn't spell; (B) I had no idea what they were used for; and (C) leaked grease.—*Erma Bombeck*

. . .

For Christmas, my wife gave me a gift that had thousands of dollars written all over it. It was a handful of Wanted posters.

I know some parents who were very smart. They bought their kids some batteries for Christmas and put a sign on them that said: "Toys Not Included."

The crowds in department stores are horrifying this time of year, but I had a pleasant time shopping the other day. That means I finished in the same clothes I started in.

Christmas is the time to eat, drink, and be merry, because starting tomorrow, you'll be doing nothing else except watching bowl games.

Of course, football is a contact sport . . . just like Christmas shopping.

Christmas is that time of year when everybody is happy, cheerful, bright, and merry. It's like any weekend at a fraternity house.

The Christmas season is starting to last longer than the basketball season.

The stores love it when the bells we hear at Christmas are from a cash register.

Early Christmas is great for kids. They can sit on Santa's knee, tell him they've been a good little boy, then go home and have three months of hell-raising before the presents arrive.

The stores are saying this year, "It's better to give than to receive. So, give me your cash, your checks, or your credit cards."

We got the kids something nice for Christmas—their own apartment.

NEW YEAR'S EVE

New Year's Eve, "where auld acquaintance be forgot"—unless those tests come back positive.—*Jay Leno*

. . .

New Year's Eve is a night when we all sing "Auld Lang Syne" from the heart, which isn't easy, since none of us knows what it means.

New Year's Eve is that night when we should all take one serious moment to tell each other how silly we all look in those party hats.

The morning after the New Year's Eve party is when you wake up to find the old year erased from your memory
. . . along with your name and where you left your car.

You know you're getting too old for wild New Year's Eve parties when you meet the Old Year on his way out and he looks younger than you do.

The nice thing about wild New Year's Eve parties is that when you wake up the next morning, you know that from that point on, the year has got to get better.

New Year's Eve is a functional holiday. After Thanksgiving and Christmas, this is the night that you finally wash down the turkey.

I once wanted to become an atheist, but I gave it up. Not enough holidays.
—*Henny Youngman*

New Year's resolutions are like the glass in fire alarms—they're only made to be broken.

Making New Year's resolutions is like holding onto a hot coal. It takes courage to try it, but it feels so damn good when you drop it.

I made a New Year's resolution to be kind, considerate, and nice. Then I decided, nah, I'd rather be myself.

New Year's resolutions are the only things in the world that are broken faster than the rules in a wrestling match.

I killed two birds with one stone this year; I gave up New Year's resolutions for Lent.

I know one guy who watched so much football on television on New Year's Day that his wife finally came in and gave him the two-minute warning on their marriage.

I know one friend who glues himself to the television set to watch football all New Year's Day. Last January it took him three days to get the AstroTurf stains off the tip of his nose.

It's always sad to ring out the old year. It means you can't get any more deductions on your tax returns.

BIRTHDAYS

My wife wanted a foreign convertible for her birthday. I got her a rickshaw.—*Henny Youngman*

I never know what to get my father for his birthday. I gave him $100 and said, "Buy yourself something that will make your life easier." So he went out and bought a present for my mother.—*Rita Rudner*

I walked into a store and said, "This is my wife's birthday. I'd like to buy her a beautiful fountain pen." The clerk said, "A little surprise, huh?" I said, "Yeah. She's expecting a Cadillac."—*Henny Youngman*

MARLENE: Last night I threw myself a surprise birthday party.
SARAH: If you threw it yourself, what was the surprise?
MARLENE: That my birthday is not until next February.

I'm such a famous person that my birthday has been declared a national holiday. If you don't believe me, just ask George Washington. He was born on the same day.

My wife said, "That gift you bought me for my 35th birthday was perfect." I said, "It should be. This is the fifth year in a row that I've bought something for your 35th birthday."

My grandfather's birthday party was postponed on account of rain. It was indoors. But he's so old that all the candles on his cake set off the sprinkler system.

You know you're getting old when one year between birthdays is not enough time to blow out all the candles on your cake.

I'm not ashamed of growing older. I always tell people my correct age on my birthday—when it rolls around every three or four years.

What ought to be done to the man who invented the celebration of anniversaries? Mere killing would be too light.—*Mark Twain*

. . .

On our anniversary, my wife told me, "I know I married you for better, for worse, for richer, for poorer, but I've changed my mind. I'm ready now for better and richer."

My wife and I got divorced on our anniversary. That's a pretty nice anniversary gift—half of everything I own.

My wife and I have been married for 12 years with time off for good behavior.

Our kids threw a surprise 25th anniversary party for us. It was a real surprise since we were divorced four years ago.

On our anniversary, I told my wife I was very proud to be married to the same woman for 25 years. She said, "After 25 years of being married to you, I'm not quite the same woman."

The first anniversary is paper. So on that day, my wife had me served.

On our anniversary, my wife and I went back to the hotel where we had had our honeymoon 25 years before. It was rundown, too.

I told my bride she gets more beautiful with each passing year. As an anniversary gift, she gave me a pair of glasses.

It's not the gift that counts; it's the thought behind it. That's kind of what I told my spouse on our last anniversary: "I *thought* I got you something."

My mother told me on her 60th wedding anniversary that marriage gets easier as you get older. She said, "There are many things I can't stand about your father, but I'll be damned if I can remember what they are."

One year, I forgot our anniversary. For the rest of the year, my wife forgot my name.

. . . And to set a place for me at dinner.

 **PARTIES**

Nothing is more irritating than not being invited to a party you wouldn't be caught dead at.—*Bill Vaughan*

I hate parties. I'm always answering questions like, "You said you were a friend of *whose* ?"—*Rodney Dangerfield*

I remember one party was called off because I *was* in town.
—*Rodney Dangerfield*

I once went to a masquerade party wearing boxer shorts. I have terrible varicose veins, so I went as a road map.—*Woody Allen*

A cocktail party is a gathering where sandwiches and friends are cut into little pieces.—*Milton Berle*

• • •

It was a great cocktail party. We killed three pitchers of martinis and seven reputations.

Good advice for cocktail parties: If you can't say something nice about someone, just hold your drink, and listen to those who can't, either.

Many cocktail parties are a group of people having a lousy time trying to have a good time.

A stranger came up to me at a cocktail party and said, "Who do you know at this party?" I said, "Absolutely no one, and I'm trying to keep it that way."

I think I had too much to drink at the party. When I put my foot in my mouth, it came out pickled.

I asked my wife if I got too loud and obnoxious at the party. She said, "Let's put it this way: It was the kind of party where a good time was had by one."

A bald head comes in handy for costume parties. I just polish it and go as a lighthouse.

I went to one cocktail party that was really a masquerade party. Everyone was disguised as someone who wanted to be there.

A gentleman came to a costume party absolutely naked. He said, "I'm dressed as Adam." The host said, "Where's Eve?" He said, "I was hoping to meet her here."

I went to one costume party dressed as Joan of Arc. They set my place for dinner *on* the barbecue.

Twenty-two of my friends and I went to a costume party dressed as circus clowns. That way we could all go in one car.

STAR-SPANGLED

Patriotism

Fourth of July

Life, Liberty & the

Pursuit of Happiness

PATRIOTISM

It will take America two more wars to learn the words to our National Anthem.—*Will Rogers*

At home, I have a map of the United States—actual size. I spent all last summer folding it.—*Steven Wright*

It is a point of pride for the American male to keep the same size Jockey shorts for his entire life.—*Bill Cosby*

I have an American Legion dog. He stops at every post.—*Milton Berle*

Whenever you hear a man speak of his love for his country, it is a sign that he expects to be paid for it.—*H. L. Mencken*

I'm still recovering from a shock. I was nearly drafted. It's not that I mind fighting for my country, but they called me at a ridiculous time: in the middle of a war.—*Jackie Mason*

A yuppie wouldn't salute the flag if it wasn't 100% cotton.
—*Mark Russell*

America is the only country where you can go on the air and kid politicians—and where politicians go on the air and kid the people.
—*Groucho Marx*

Ask not what your country can do for you, but how much it's going to cost you for them to do it.

I love God and country in that order . . . because God doesn't charge taxes.

My uncle is a great patriot, but he's also very lazy. His goal in life is to write a National Anthem that we can all sit down to.

My uncle says that America is the only country that he would ever live in. It's not that he's a patriot; his passport has been taken away from him.

I have an uncle who is very proud of the fact that he has never voted for any politician. He says, "It only encourages them."

I have another uncle who says that America is the most beautiful land he's ever seen in the entire country.

My other uncle hates taxes. When they play the National Anthem, he puts his hand over his wallet.

My uncle is a great patriot. He says he loves all forty-eight states. His heart is big, but his geography book is terribly outdated.

I have a friend who is a California kid at heart, but he happens to live in Kansas. His ambition is to someday go surfing on the amber waves of grain.

I have one question: If America is filled with amber waves of grain, how come cereal costs so much?

I have an uncle who is a great patriot but a lousy judge of tattoo artists. He has a tattoo over his chest that reads, *"E pluribus unub ."*

FOURTH of JULY

We only had one minor problem on July 4th. We had to ask the kids to turn down their stereo so that we could hear the fireworks.
—*Robert Orben*

. . .

Every Fourth of July, we'd give my uncle a hotfoot while he was sleeping. His language when he woke up was the only fireworks we could afford.

The Fourth of July is a tribute to America. Thanks to American politicians, we cannot only put over 200 candles on our cake, but we also have enough hot air to blow them out.

It's a funny thing about our nation. July 4th is its birthday, but April 15th is when it collects the presents.

Can you imagine? If our Founding Fathers could see this country today, they'd look at the smog and think the English were trying to win the Revolution with germ warfare.
. . . They'd look at all the nudity in our movies and wonder why Betsy

"Oh, give me a home where the buffalo roam, . . ." and I'll show you a house full of dirt.
—*Marty Allen*

Ross gave up sewing.

. . . They'd see all our traffic jams and be glad that Paul Revere rode a horse.

. . . They'd see the costumes that some of our teenage girls wear and know why our national anthem begins "Oh say, can you see . . ."

You know the rarest thing in the world? An ant who oversleeps on the Fourth of July.

There are two sounds you hear an awful lot on July 4th: firecrackers going off and ants licking their chops.

Everybody eats outdoors on this holiday. It's an unwritten law: the Fourth of July is the oven's day off.

The Fourth of July comes in the middle of the summer, but it's not the longest day of the year. It only seems that way when you're trying to light the charcoal.

We have some of the worst chefs in the world cooking outdoors on July 4th. If you don't believe me, just watch the flies in the evening. They buzz around the medicine chest.

My dad always used to cook outdoors on the Fourth of July. *Medium rare* meant you got your steak before the fire department came.

You can always tell a good barbecue chef. He's the one who still has eyebrows when he's done.

The biggest cause of injury at the Fourth-of-July picnic is food inhalation.

If you really want to eat a good meal outdoors on the Fourth of July, be a mosquito.

LIFE, LIBERTY & THE PURSUIT OF HAPPINESS

Liberty don't work as good in practice as it does in speech.—*Will Rogers*

Liberty means responsibility. That is why most men dread it.
—*George Bernard Shaw*

A husband is a man who lost his liberty in the pursuit of happiness.
—*Milton Berle*

Happiness? A good cigar, a good meal, and a good woman—or a bad woman. It depends on how much happiness you can handle.
—*George Burns*

Money can't buy happiness. It just helps you look for it in more places.
—*Milton Berle*

It's pretty hard to tell what does bring happiness; both poverty and wealth have failed.—*Kin Hubbard*

I never knew what real happiness was until I got married. And then it was too late.—*Max Kauffmann*

Some people bring happiness wherever they go; you bring happiness whenever you go.—*Henny Youngman*

. . .

The most precious thing we have is life. Yet it has absolutely no trade-in value.

We all treasure life. In fact, most of us carry it with us to our deathbed.

Nathan Hale is famous for saying, "I regret I have but one life to give for my country." His cat made the same speech nine times.

Life is what we do while we're waiting for the other shoe to drop.

It's amazing the rights people will give up to be free.

Liberty is the right to complain that we don't have enough freedom.

Have you ever noticed? The Statue of Liberty is not allowed to move.

I've been engaged in the pursuit of happiness all my life. When I got it, I found out I couldn't afford it.

We're all free to pursue happiness for as long as we wish, or we can just take a cash settlement.

Our Constitution guarantees us the right to the pursuit of happiness. Unfortunately, we do have to provide our own funds.

Our forefathers guaranteed us the right to the pursuit of happiness. They should have given us a few clues as to where to look.

Will I ever attain happiness in this life? If Sharon Stone responds favorably to my letter, I might.

NIGHT ON THE TOWN

Television

Books

Music

Movies

Ballet

Opera

# TELEVISION

Television is a *medium* . . . so-called because it's neither rare nor well done.—*Ernie Kovacs*

Who says we didn't have controversial subjects on TV back then? Remember *Bonanza*? It was about three guys in high heels living together.—*Milton Berle*

I just got my TV set insured. If it breaks down, they send me a pair of binoculars so I can watch my neighbor's set.—*Henny Youngman*

If it wasn't for electricity, we'd all be watching television by candlelight.—*George Gobel*

I've been watching so many Westerns on television, the legs under my living room chair are permanently bowed.—*Jack Carter*

Television is like your wife. It's home and it's free.—*Slappy White*

. . .

Television is nature's way of telling us we should have gone out and done something enjoyable this evening.

Television is something to do without actually doing anything.

They've improved practically everything on television, except the programming.

With cable, some people get a selection of 100 different channels. That means 100 times every half hour they get to say, "See what else is on."

Calling television "entertainment" is like calling falling off a cliff "transportation."

Television is radio without the imagination.

There are three kinds of television programming: good, bad, and good and bad.

Home-shopping shows are very big on television and very convenient. You can now go broke in the comfort of your own living room.

Television used to exhibit bad taste. Now, thanks to home shopping, you can have it delivered.

Talk shows have been popular on TV for about 15 years now. Pretty soon they're going to say something.

Talk shows are informational. They discuss in depth topics that are of interest to no one.

Talk shows can be very educational. For much of my life, I was under the mistaken assumption there were only two sexes.

Television will never replace the newspaper. You can't wrap a fish in it.

TV talk shows ran out of things to talk about years ago. They just haven't stopped talking yet.

BOOKS

I can't understand why a person would take a year to write a novel when he can easily buy one for a few dollars.—*Fred Allen*

From the moment I picked your book up until I laid it down, I was convulsed with laughter. Someday I intend to read it.—*Groucho Marx*

This must be a gift book. That is to say, a book which you wouldn't take on any other terms.—*Dorothy Parker*

Just got back from the hospital. I was in a speed-reading accident.
—*Steven Wright*

First time I read the dictionary I thought it was a poem about everything.—*Steven Wright*

I have given up reading books. I find it takes my mind off myself.
—*Oscar Levant*

The covers of this book are too far apart.—*Ambrose Bierce*

Be careful about reading health books. You may die of a misprint.
—*Mark Twain*

I have one hundred fifty books, but I have no bookcase. Nobody would lend me a bookcase.—*Henny Youngman*

I went to a bookstore, and I asked the clerk where the self-help section was. She said, "If I told you, that would defeat the whole purpose."
—*Brian Kiley*

. . .

I love to read a good book before going to sleep, because after going to sleep I keep forgetting to turn the pages.

Books can take you to anyplace in the world, and they have more leg room than most airplanes.

Some say dog is man's best friend; I say books are. You don't have to walk them or clean up after them.

Two things can ruin a good book for me: having someone tell me the ending or dropping it into the bathwater.

I read a book on levitation the other day. I couldn't put it down.

I read a good book on improving your memory. It was called, uh . . .

I had a book on improving your memory. I read it twice. I forgot I read it the first time.

I always read the last chapter of murder mysteries first. I know who did it, but I have no idea what they did.

I'm a very slow reader. By the time I get to the end of a murder mystery, it doesn't matter who did it. The statute of limitations has run out.

I had a friend who once tried to read the local phone book from cover to cover, but he kept losing track of the characters.

I picked up a self-help book that was so complicated that I had to get someone to help me read it.

I bought a book about near-death experiences, but I took it back. I didn't like the ending. . . . It didn't seem complete.

 **MUSIC**

I've played the harmonica ever since I was big enough to defend myself.
—*Herb Shriner*

Modern music hasn't been around too long and hopefully won't be.
—*Victor Borge*

Jack Benny is the only fiddler who makes you feel that the strings would sound better back in the cat.—*Fred Allen*

I haven't heard singing like that since I was over at the zoo and the moose sat down on the porcupine.—*Amos 'n' Andy*

The Steinway people have asked me to announce that this is a Baldwin piano.—*Victor Borge*

My father once tried to play "Flight of the Bumblebee" on the tuba. Blew his liver through the horn.—*Woody Allen*

I see the Beatles have arrived from England. They were forty pounds overweight, and that was just their hair.—*Bob Hope*

. . .

When he plays the piano, I want to get up and dance. Anything is better than just sitting there and listening.

They laughed when I sat down to play. I was facing away from the piano.

He plays the French horn so badly that it comes out sounding like Greek.

When he plays the trumpet, the trumpet usually wins.

When he plays classical music, it gives Beethoven a reason to be glad he's deaf.

When she sings, she hits notes so high that only dogs can hear them. As far as I'm concerned, that's the dogs' problem.

He plays "Flight of the Bumblebee" as if he has already been stung.

When I play the guitar, I can clear a room faster than a smoke alarm.

He can only play two songs on the piano. One is "Old McDonald Had a Farm" and the other one isn't.

When he plays "The Blue Danube," you kind of hope he'll throw himself into it.

Some people can play and make you appreciate music. When he plays, he makes you appreciate earplugs.

An incurable music lover is someone who will buy a set of drums for his own kid.

MOVIES

If my film makes one more person miserable, I'll feel I've done my job. —*Woody Allen*

The Academy Awards are definitely fixed. The Best Actress award is always won by a woman.—*Groucho Marx*

. . .

It's fun . . . a good movie, a large box of popcorn, a soft drink . . . what better way to spend 30 or 40 dollars?

Of course, the large size of popcorn is a very good buy, because once you eat the popcorn, you can have the container made into a summer home.

You used to be able to go into the theater and buy a normal-size chocolate bar. Now they sell it by the acre.

Movies make a lot more money today than they used to. Of course, with what you pay for a ticket today, you used to be able to buy a home back then.

It used to be that if a film made 7 or 8 million dollars, it was a hit. Now that's what the star's agent gets.

The movie industry made a fortune. The MGM lion doesn't growl anymore. He just smiles and counts.

How about all those horror films! Who ever thought we'd see the day when an actor would write on his resume: "Can operate a chain saw."

Years ago, the worst violence was a pie in the face. Nowadays you rarely get to keep your face through the entire movie.

Gangster movies are kind of self-defeating. It's hard to prove that crime doesn't pay when you're paying $9.50 a pop to see it.

Years ago, movies used to have a story line. Today all they need is a choice of weapons and a list of victims.

All these new action-adventure films have a standard story line—boy meets girl, boy loses girl, boy blows up everybody in the picture.

There are a lot of movies out now aimed at youngsters. They have a special rating. Parents are not admitted unless they have a teenager there to explain it to them.

BALLET

You go to the ballet and you see girls dancing on their toes. Why don't they just get taller girls?—*Greg Ray*

I was a ballerina. I had to quit after I injured a groin muscle. It wasn't mine.—*Rita Rudner*

I didn't dig ballet. The last time I went with friends—there was a lot of money bet on the swan to live.—*Woody Allen*

. . .

Some people say that ballet tells a story. Those are probably the people who stay awake for it.

Male dancers wear what they call ballet tights. If anything, that's an understatement.

Those costumes are so tight that if you have a tattoo, you have to wear it outside your leotards.

Ballet demands discipline, skill, athleticism, perseverance, and courage. And that's just to get into the tights.

Ballet dancers always seem to be jumping up in the air. That's because in those tight costumes, it's preferable to bending over.

It's very relaxing to sit in the audience and watch people dance ballet. That's because no matter what you're wearing, it's more comfortable than what they're wearing.

I never danced ballet. The closest I ever came was as a kid walking over hot asphalt in my bare feet.

Some people go to the ballet for the music, some for the dance. And many go because they lost an argument with their spouse.

It's not easy to do a *pas de deux,* a *tour en l'air,* a *brisé,* or a *penché.* A normal person could pull a muscle just trying to spell them.

Probably more American men would enjoy ballet if they could watch it with their shoes off and a six-pack of beer.
. . . And being able to bet on it wouldn't hurt.

I don't understand ballet. I don't understand calculus either, but I've never paid 50 bucks a ticket to go watch calculus.

OPERA

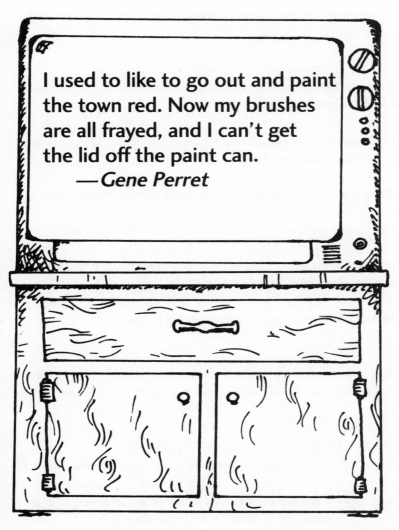

I used to like to go out and paint the town red. Now my brushes are all frayed, and I can't get the lid off the paint can.
—*Gene Perret*

Opera in English is, in the main, just about as sensible as baseball in Italian.—*H. L. Mencken*

When an opera star sings her head off, she usually improves her appearance.—*Victor Borge*

I go to the opera whether I need the sleep or not.—*Henny Youngman*

. . .

If I wanted to hear people sing in a foreign language, I would have been born in a foreign country.

I go to the opera house because it makes my wife happy. I just wish that sometimes she'd come with me.

The thing I hate most about opera singing is that it usually wakes me up.

I would enjoy a good night at the opera, if there were such a thing.

I enjoy going to the opera. I also enjoy coming home again. It's sitting there through the whole thing that gets me.

My spouse takes me to the opera so often that I've learned to snore in Italian.

My wife gets upset with me because every time she wants to go to the opera, I want to stay home. So I've offered a compromise. I'll go halfway there.

I've finally figured out why operas are all in a foreign language. That's so the guy who wrote them would understand them.

To me, a night at the opera is watching a play I don't like, sung in a language I don't understand, wearing a tuxedo that doesn't fit.

Opera is rap music for highbrows.

I go to the opera regularly. I'm going to keep going until I understand what's happening.

THE BEEP ON THE ROAD TO SUCCESS

Success

Opportunity

Failure

Off to Work

Some Odd Jobs

Modern Technology

Computers

Beepers

SUCCESS

If at first you don't succeed, try, try again. Then quit. No use being a damn fool about it.—*W. C. Fields*

They say behind every successful man, there's a woman.
Take a good look at me. Can you picture what I've got behind me?
—*Rodney Dangerfield*

There's no secret about success. Did you ever know a successful man who didn't tell you all about it?—*Kin Hubbard*

I was voted the Dropout Most Likely to Succeed.—*Jan Murray*

That's all there is to success is satisfaction.—*Will Rogers*

If at first you don't succeed, cheat.—*Red Buttons*

The man with a new idea is a crank until the idea succeeds.—*Mark Twain*

All you need in this life is ignorance and confidence, and then success is sure.—*Mark Twain*

We can't all be heroes, because somebody has to sit on the curb and clap as they go by.—*Will Rogers*

I know you won't let success go to your head. Nothing else has.

You've worked hard for everything you have. You obviously didn't get it on personality.

If at first you don't succeed, try, try again. Failures like you need something to keep them occupied.

There's only one thing keeping me from being a success—abject failure.

The one thing my mother wanted was a successful son.
I did my part. I urged her to have more children.

If at first you don't succeed, become a consultant and teach someone else how to do it.

I consider myself a success because I always wanted to be the biggest failure in the world.

Everybody wants to be more successful than the next guy. So try to stand next to some guy who's not doing that well.

I've been a success and I've been a failure. Failure
doesn't take as long.
. . . But it's more enduring.

If you want to avoid traffic, get on the road to success.

A friend of mine started a business teaching people how to be successful.
He had to; he needed the money.

OPPORTUNITY

I was seldom able to see an opportunity until it had ceased to be one.
—*Mark Twain*

Some people don't recognize opportunity when it knocks because it
comes.—*H. L. Mencken*

. . .

Opportunity only knocks once, which means it would make a lousy
Avon lady.

What I can't figure out is: how come opportunity knocks once, but
the postman always rings twice?

Whenever someone tells you, "This is the opportunity of a lifetime," ask if
they're referring to your lifetime or theirs.

It's so unfair. Opportunity only knocks once, but my car knocks every
time I drive it over 40 miles an hour.

My brother-in-law is so lazy, every time there's a knock on the door, he
pretends he's not home. He's afraid it might be opportunity.

The young worker said, "All I want is an opportunity," but he wasn't
being truthful. He wanted a salary, too.

He said, "All I want is an opportunity to show you what I can do." He showed us, and now he's looking for an opportunity someplace else.

It's a cop-out to say that opportunity only knocks once. There are plenty of seashells in the world, but how many of them knock on your door more than once?

Opportunity knocked at my door once. I must have been in the shower at the time.

Anytime someone tells you they're offering you the opportunity of a lifetime, be careful. It'll probably cost your life savings.

Many people go out and become a success while others are sitting home waiting for opportunity to knock.

Opportunity is nature's way of saying, "Hey, if you don't make it, dummy, it's your own fault."

 **FAILURE**

Nothing is all wrong. Even a clock that stops is right twice a day. —*Morey Amsterdam*

This guy is such a loser that he gives failure a bad name.—*Joey Adams*

If at first you don't succeed, failure may be your thing.—*Milton Berle*

I am not a failure; I'm a success that hasn't happened yet.
. . . My credit card company says they're not canceling my card; they're just holding it until I happen.

Some endeavors are doomed to failure, like trying to jump across a well in two jumps.

My uncle has a bright philosophy. He says, "I am not a failure. I'm a success who has no money and can't get a job."

I picked up a self-help book that said on the cover, "There is no such thing as failure." Then two clerks chased me out of the store because of my failure to pay for the book.

A wise soldier once said that retreat is just fighting in the opposite direction. By the same token, I feel I'm not a failure; I'm just very successful at not getting what I want.

Some say that failure is a state of mind. I'm in the state of mind that I haven't paid any of my bills in over 4 months.

My dad always taught me: "There's no such thing as failure." Then one day, he asked to see my report card. I told him, "There's no such thing as my report card."

Some sage once advised that every failure leads to an eventual success. He was right. I failed to stay on my diet, and now I successfully can't fit into any of my clothes.

The blowhard's success formula: If at first you don't succeed, lie, lie again.

Failure is nothing to be ashamed of. Just look upon it as success that happened for somebody else.

If at first you don't succeed, pretend that's not what you were trying to do in the first place.

Anyone who believes there is no such thing as failure has never tried to play golf.

Half the people like to work, and the other half don't. Or maybe it's the other way around.—*Sam Levenson*

Anyone can do any amount of work, provided it isn't the work he is supposed to be doing at that moment.—*Robert Benchley*

It is better to have a permanent income than to be fascinating.
—*Oscar Wilde*

The man with the best job in the country is the Vice President. All he has to do is get up every morning and say, "How's the President?"
—*Will Rogers*

He works 8 hours a day and sleeps 8 hours a day—the same 8 hours.
—*Milton Berle*

People who work sitting down get paid more than people who work standing up.—*Ogden Nash*

My brother-in-law has an allergy. He's allergic to work.
—*Henny Youngman*

He's a real workaholic. You mention work, he gets drunk.
—*Rodney Dangerfield*

I think the easiest job in the world has to be coroner. Surgery on dead people: what's the worst thing that could happen?—*Dennis Miller*

. . .

As if getting up in the morning isn't bad enough, it has to be followed by going to work.

Getting up and going to work in the morning—what a waste of 8 good hours of sleep.

I don't mind going to work in the morning. I don't mind coming home, either. It's the 8 hours in between that get my goat.

I have a simple definition of work: anything that has to be done standing up.

I don't like to drink too much coffee in the morning. If I do, I toss and turn all through the workday.

I like driving the crowded freeways to work in the morning. It's a chance to see new faces and learn a lot of new hand signals.

Some people can't wait to get to work on Monday morning. They're the ones who won the football pool over the weekend.

Some experts claim work can be fun if you make a game of it. So I did—hide-and-seek.
. . . I don't show up at the office, and they have to come find me.

The 24-hour day works out perfectly. We get 8 hours for sleep, 8 hours for work, and 8 hours to complain about too much work and not enough sleep.

The first thing I do when I get to the office is have a cup of coffee before getting down to serious work. That convinces me that what this country really needs is a good 8-hour cup of coffee.

The only good thing about going to work is that it's a prerequisite to coming home from work.

One of my first office jobs was cleaning the windows on the envelopes.
—*Rita Rudner*

For a while I had a series of very unusual jobs. I was a night watchman in a day camp, a deckhand on a submarine, a traffic director in a phone booth, and a cruise director on a Ferris wheel.—*Jackie Vernon*

I used to be a translator for bad mimes.—*Steven Wright*

He was a falsies manufacturer. He lived off the flat of the land.
—*Groucho Marx*

My brother-in-law just got a job as a lifeguard in a car wash.
—*Henny Youngman*

I used to be a proofreader for a skywriting company.—*Steven Wright*

. . .

That might be one of the easiest jobs of all time—being a bouncer in hell.

MODERN TECHNOLOGY

My father was replaced at work with a gadget that's about this big that does everything my father does, but better. The depressing thing is my mother went out and bought one.—*Woody Allen*

America is angry that we lost our technological edge. But we're not a scientific country anymore. Think about it: We couldn't even go metric.
—*Bill Maher*

. . .

The world is getting too technologically advanced. I was just talking about that with my clone the other day. . . .

Today, everything is done by machines. The world is not going to come to an end. It's just going to sit around a long time waiting for the repairman.

Technology is moving so fast nowadays that it's tough on scientists. By the time you invent anything today it has already become obsolete.

We're doing a lot of things today that we shouldn't be doing—just because we can.

. . . And some things that aren't even worth doing, we're doing more quickly.

Technology has its drawbacks. I've yet to meet a Native American who couldn't send a smoke signal because of a power blackout.

There's only one thing left for science to invent: something useful that doesn't beep or flash.

You know, it's a shame the Big Bang didn't happen at this moment in time. We could have videotaped it.

Every form of communication has been vastly improved by modern technology, except conversation.

They finally came up with the perfect office computer. If it makes a mistake, it blames another computer.
— *Milton Berle*

COMPUTERS

Man, endowed with that incredible computer known as the human brain, has used it to invent an electronic brain.—*Sam Levenson*

The computer didn't eliminate red tape; it only perforated it.
—*Sam Levenson*

I hate computers. When I went to school, all I had was a pencil and the kid next to me.
. . . And I think if he had applied himself, I could have been somebody.
—*Allen Stephan*

• • •

Computers used to be user-friendly. Now they're getting downright flirtatious.

Computers are fast. I can now make ten times the mistakes I used to make manually.

Just think, if Shakespeare had had a computer, he probably would have accidentally erased *A Midsummer Night's Dream.*
. . . And *Troilus and Cressida* would have been kicked out the first time he ran through the spell-check.

With computers we can now do a full day's work in one hour. Of course, it takes us seven hours to figure out what we did.

Remember, computers can't think for themselves. They're just like any other worker in your office.

Since the introduction of computers into the workplace, I'm now the second smartest thing sitting at my desk.

My computer was acting strangely, but the repairman figured out what the problem was. He said there was a nut loose at the keyboard.

Computers are not intelligent. If they were, they wouldn't let us humans anywhere near them.

They say computers can't think, but I have one that does. It thinks it's broken.

I bought a new program that helps me figure out my family budget. Firstthing it figured out was that I couldn't afford this program.

With the computer, I still do dumb things, but now I can list them in either alphabetical or chronological order.

The computer is a poor substitute for intelligence, but then, aren't we all?

 **BEEPERS**

My boss wanted me to wear a beeper, but I refused. I don't want anything else on my body that could fall off.

My boss said, "I want to be able to reach you no matter where you travel." I said, "Then come with me."
... "You can drive."

I don't like beepers. If I have strange noises coming from my body unexpectedly, I want it to mean I have indigestion.

I put the wrong size of batteries in the beeper that I wear on my belt. The first call I got blew my shoes off.

My beeper went off in the middle of the opera. Four of the spear carriers threw them at me.

I have a terrible job—important enough for a beeper, but not important enough for a raise.

A friend of mine is very cheap; his beeper is on a party line.

I think my beeper is a little too powerful. Every time I get a message, my garage door opens.

One advertisement said, "Get a beeper and never miss an important call." I just sit by the phone, and I never miss not having a beeper.

My dog has a special beeper. He knows which dogs are in heat over a five-state area.

My secretary called me on my beeper to tell me that I left my beeper in the office.

MONEY

Wealth

Stock Market

Expensive

Inflation

Saving Money

Money Troubles

WEALTH

A man who has $11 million is just as happy as a man who has . . . $12 million.—*Joe E. Lewis*

Two very rich people got divorced, and their lawyers lived happily ever after.—*Milton Berle*

He's so rich he sends care packages to Nelson Rockefeller.—*Bob Hope*

He's so rich his apartment has four area codes.—*Jack E. Leonard*

. . .

So many people want to get rich quick. I'm not like that. I want to get rich *now.*

I know a guy who's so rich that if he ever goes broke, it'll take two trips.

Everything this guy touches turns to gold. That's why he can't eat finger foods.

This guy is so rich his butler has a chauffeur.

This guy is so rich he's got money he hasn't even had to lie about yet.

I know one guy who is so status-conscious that everything he does has got to be the richest. He even goes to a church with bucket pews.

Someday my ship will come in. With my luck, when it does, it'll probably break down my dock.

I have a friend who has plenty of money, but is he happy? I don't know because since he got rich, he doesn't hang around with me.

I'm pretty close to being a millionaire; I'm only seven figures away.

Oh, sure, I'd like to have all the money in the world, but could I afford to pay the taxes on it?

One bad thing about having all the money in the world—who would you borrow from?

A poor person can have a maid, a butler, and a chauffeur, too. That's if he can find three people dumb enough to work for a percentage.

The rich get richer and the poor get poorer. Me? I've got just enough to get bad credit ratings.

I don't know how he got all his money. Most people who have that much got it by declaring war against the United States and then losing.

Someday I'd like to be rich enough to get out of all the trouble my poverty got me into.

It's been said, "If you cast your bread upon the water, it will come back to you a hundredfold." That's pretty good advice, if you like to eat soggy sandwiches.

Nobody knows how much he's worth. His money doesn't stay still long enough to be counted.

But as rich as he is, he uses his money for a good cause. . . to get more.

STOCK MARKET

When Coolidge was president, men bought stocks who had never even bought toothpaste before.—*Will Rogers*

There are two times in a man's life when he should not speculate: when he can afford it and when he can't.—*Mark Twain*

The past few weeks, Wall Street has gone into one tailspin after another. You would pick up the morning paper, read the stock report, and wouldn't think there were that many minus signs in the world.—*Will Rogers*

My father was a very successful businessman, but he was ruined in the stock-market crash.
. . . A big stockbroker jumped out the window and fell on his pushcart.
—*Jackie Mason*

A stockbroker is a man who runs your fortune into a shoe-string.
—*Alexander Woollcott*

· · ·

I called my broker yesterday, and he put me on hold. By the time he got back on the phone, I had nothing left to talk to him about.

I lost so much money in the market this year that I can afford to tell the truth on my tax return.

Wall Street is in a slump. It doesn't become a catastrophe until it's their own money they start losing.

Wall Street is expecting the worst. The last time I saw my broker, he was wearing a crash helmet.

The stock market performed so badly today that I went down to Wall Street and laid a wreath on my money.

Wall Street must be doing badly today. I tried to call my broker and he wouldn't accept the charges.

I tried to check how my stocks were doing in the newspaper. I had to keep switching back and forth from the financial pages to the obituaries.

I lost so much money so fast in the stock market today, my wallet has skid marks on it.

The only things I read in the newspaper anymore are the comic pages and the stock market—the funnies and the saddies.

I called my stockbroker and asked how badly my investments were doing. He said, "In five seconds, your credit cards will self-destruct."

It's not real hard to find my stocks on the financial page. They're the ones that are trimmed in black.

My stocks are doing very badly right about now. I used to shower every day; now I take a bath, too.

When I first heard how badly the stock market was doing, I tried to call my broker, but his ledge was busy.

The stock market went down fast, and a lot of people in Beverly Hills lost quite a bit of money. People there now have their chauffeurs drop them off at a soup kitchen.

The stock market fell so badly it even hurt Hollywood. Tinseltown can't even afford real tinsel.

Johnny Carson was hurt real badly by the stock-market decline. It's the most money he's lost while he's still been married to the same woman.

EXPENSIVE

Money is better than poverty, if only for financial reasons.—*Woody Allen*

Politics has become so expensive that it takes a lot of money even to be defeated.—*Will Rogers*

At today's prices, you're lucky if you can make one end meet.
—*Milton Berle*

Among the things that money can't buy is what it used to.
—*Max Kaufman*

Funerals are so expensive. When my uncle died, my aunt couldn't afford a casket; so she bought him a suit with six handles.

Extreme wealth used to be a status symbol. Now it's a necessity just to make ends meet.

You go into a realtor today and say, "What can you show me for $50,000?" They show you the door.

Millionaire used to mean a rich man. Today it just means a guy who might own his own home.

A Rolex watch costs between $4,000 and $20,000. I don't want to know the time that bad.
. . . It's cheaper to carry a pocket full of quarters and just dial 555–TIME.

Everyone should have a roof over his head. If you also want walls and a floor, you may be getting out of your price range.

Women are worried about who's going to care for their kids while they work. That shouldn't be a problem much longer. With today's housing costs, even the kids will have to find jobs.

Sporting events are getting expensive. Soon the fans will have to decide whether to go to the game or send their kids to college.

INFLATION

Inflation is when the buck doesn't stop anywhere.—*Robert Orben*

Inflation has hit everything. Pillow down is up, Macy's Basement is now on the fourth floor, and pumpernickel is now pumperdime.—*Marty Brill*

Inflation is when you're wealthy and you no longer can afford the things you bought when you were poor.—*Robert Orben*

Inflation—that's when prices go from reasonable to expensive to "How much have you got with you?"—*Bob Hope*

Americans are getting stronger. Twenty years ago it took two people to carry ten dollars' worth of groceries. Today a five-year-old can do it.

—*Henny Youngman*

I joined an organization that fights inflation. An hour after I joined, they raised the dues.—*Milton Berle*

I don't mind going back to daylight saving time. With inflation, the hour will be the only thing I've saved this year.—*Victor Borge*

Inflation! When Congress becomes ten percent efficient, why, that is inflation.—*Will Rogers*

Times are so bad nowadays; even people who don't intend to pay ain't buying.—*Slappy White*

I figure inflation is really here. I gave my nephew a nickel and he asked, "What is this thing—a medal?"—*Pat Cooper*

. . .

Whoever said "Whatever goes up must come down" has not bothered to check the price of houses lately.

Inflation has driven the value of our money down so much that now even muggers won't accept cash.

Inflation means if you put off 'til tomorrow what you could do today, you might not be able to afford to do it.

Inflation is when things cost more and are worth less. That also describes most souvenir shops.

Inflation is when everything you have is worth more, except you.

One way to beat inflation is if you need something today, buy it tomorrow at yesterday's prices.

Costs have gone up so much that they've changed the Lord's Prayer to "Give us this day our daily bread, plus shipping and handling."

Prices have gone up so much; nowadays only the rich can afford to act like the middle class.

One good thing about inflation: poverty is now affordable to everyone.

Inflation is terrible. Interest is worth more than money these days.

Inflation continues to go up. They used to say, "Money can't buy happiness." Today it can't even buy groceries.

Everything costs so much today that they've now come up with a wallet that fits conveniently under the seat in front of you or in the overhead compartment.

Nowadays, things cost so much that some people want to get shoplifting reduced from a misdemeanor to a necessity.

Prices are getting ridiculous. Supermarkets now have a bag boy to help you carry the money in.

Inflation is kind of hard to explain. Think of it as termites of the wallet.

Inflation means your money can't buy as much today as it did yesterday. My money can't buy anything today; I spent it all yesterday.

Look on the bright side of inflation. If you could have lived in the 18th century, you would have been rich by now.

Inflation means that when you've save up for old age, you go broke when you're middle-aged.

Inflation is getting so bad that today not even the Joneses can afford to keep up with the Joneses.

Inflation means if you're worth nothing today, you'll be worth less tomorrow.

Inflation means you can still buy a good 5-cent cigar, but it costs you $5.75.

Inflation means that this year's money will someday be worth as much as last year's calendar.

My dad said that when he was a kid, milk was only 2 cents a quart. I don't know why he didn't buy a whole lot of it then, and save it.

I don't have a savings account because . . . I don't know my mother's maiden name.—*Paula Poundstone*

I try to save my money. Who knows? Maybe one day it'll become valuable again.—*Milton Berle*

My wife will buy anything marked down. Yesterday, she tried to buy an escalator.—*Joey Bishop*

And when it comes to sales, my wife is the all-time champion. Our local supermarket now advertises sales by posters that say, "Dear Mrs. King,..."—*Alan King*

My wife makes the budget work. We do without a lot of things I don't need.—*Milton Berle*

Save a little money each month, and at the end of the year, you'll be surprised at how little you have.—*Ernest Haskins*

My father originated the limbo dance—trying to get into a pay toilet.
—*Slappy White*

My wife loves bargains. What a great shopper! One time she went out window shopping—came home with seven windows.—*Alan King*

I tried to save grocery money once, but some of the suggestions were just not practical, like "Don't shop when you're hungry," which eliminated all hours when the store was open.—*Erma Bombeck*

. . .

I've been trying to save up for a rainy day. So far I can handle a light mist.

I've been saving for a rainy day. I'm happy to say that in two more years I can buy that umbrella.

I always throw my loose change into a large vase because my mother always told me, "A penny saved is a penny urned."

Two can live as cheaply as one . . . if one of them doesn't eat.

I finally saved up enough money to do something I've been meaning to do since 1960. I bought a 1960 Cadillac.

I finally saved up enough to open a savings account at the bank. The toaster they gave me set fire to my kitchen.

I withdrew my life savings from the bank. The teller asked, "How would you like that? Heads or tails?"

I've saved for years and years. Do you know what I got? Older.

My grandparents lost their life savings by taking a cruise. What Granddad thought was a wall safe turned out to be a porthole.

I try to save by clipping coupons. Last week alone, I got about 50 to 60 paper cuts.

My bank not only pays next to nothing on my savings account, but the calendar they sent me at New Year's only has 13 days in each month.

I always carry a little cash that I call mad money. Every time I look at it, it makes me mad that I don't have more.

GEORGE: Rich, me? No, I'm a pauper.
GRACIE: Congratulations! Boy or girl?
—*George Burns and Gracie Allen*

We had so little to eat one year, I forgot how to swallow.—*Joey Bishop*

Freezing people for the future isn't a new idea; landlords discovered it years ago.—*Pat Cooper*
. . . Also, with money, you can be miserable in much better surroundings.

WORDS OF WISDOM

Progress

Philosophy

Cautious

Wacky Wisdom

A Few Crazy Thoughts

Silly Things to Ponder

PROGRESS

We do more talking progress than we do progressing.—*Will Rogers*

Happiness and contentment is progress. In fact that's all progress is.
—*Will Rogers*

Things ain't what they used to be; in fact, at our house, they never was.
—*Herb Shriner*

It's hard to get used to these changing times. I can remember when the air was clean and the sex was dirty.—*George Burns*

GEORGE: Gracie, what do you think of television?
GRACIE: I think it's wonderful. I hardly ever watch radio anymore.
—*George Burns and Gracie Allen*

When I was a boy of 14, my father was so ignorant. But when I got to be 21, I was amazed to see how much he had learned in seven years.
—*Mark Twain*

The old believe everything; the middle-aged suspect everything; the young know everything.—*Oscar Wilde*

Progress might have been all right once, but it has gone on far too long.
—*Ogden Nash*

. . .

If things keep getting better all the time, how come so many people remember the "good old days"?

Progress sometimes means we just have a faster way of doing something that was never necessary in the first place.

I hate progress. It means that everything improves over time except me.

Progress is not always good. I remember when moving pictures started talking. Now the entire audience does, too.

Progress means just when we can afford something, they make a new and better one that we can't.

They had pollution in the old days, but at least you could put it on your roses.

Have you noticed? Everything in the world keeps improving except people.

Cars can now go five times as fast as they used to, but there are twenty times more of them, so it takes twice as long to get there.

Because of progress, we all now own a toaster where the bread pops up when it's burnt.

Is it progress when we have coffee that won't keep us awake at night and television shows that won't either?

 # PHILOSOPHY

A man begins cutting his wisdom teeth the first time he bites off more than he can chew.—*Herb Caen*

To err is human, but it feels divine.—*Mae West*

Be good and you will be lonely.—*Mark Twain*

If you're going to do something tonight that you'll be sorry for tomorrow, sleep late.—*Henny Youngman*

Life is what happens to you while you're busy making other plans.
—*John Lennon*

Some people go to India to find the mystery of life. I'm still trying to figure out how to start my car.—*Rodney Dangerfield*

An uneasy conscience is a hair in the mouth.—*Mark Twain*

Honesty is the best policy, but it is not the cheapest.—*Mark Twain*

My grandfather always told me, "Don't guard your money; guard your health." While I was busy guarding my health, my grandfather stole my
—*Jackie Mason*

Let us endeavor so to live that when we come to die even the undertaker will be sorry.—*Mark Twain*

· · ·

All work and no play makes Jack a dull boy—but a helluva lot richer than you are.

My grandfather used to say I couldn't see the forest for the trees. I didn't pay much attention to him, though. He couldn't see the forest for his hangover.

The early bird, they say, catches the worm. I say, let him have it! I'll sleep in and settle for sausage and eggs.

I never understood that admonition, the early bird catches the worm. It doesn't say much for the early worm, does it?

Here are a few other little known, but wise admonitions:
. . . Never eat in a restaurant where antacid is listed on the menu as a side dish.

. . . Never entrust your life to a surgeon with more than three Band-Aids on his fingers.

. . . Never go to a plastic surgeon whose favorite artist is Picasso.

. . . Never get in line at the bank behind a person wearing a ski mask.

. . . If a band of motorcyclists all wearing black leather vests and covered with tattoos cuts you off on the highway, just think the obscenities quietly to yourself.

. . . If you have nothing good to say about someone, go on an afternoon talk show and say it anyway.

 # CAUTIOUS

I have a telescope on the peephole of my door so that I can see who's at the door for 200 miles.—*Steven Wright*

. . .

Cautious is never making the same mistake once.

I know a man who is overly cautious. He won't even walk the straight and narrow without a safety net under him.

My grandfather always said the best advice he ever heard was look before you leap. He thought it explained why there were so few blind pole-vaulters.

My grandmother was always careful never to date a man who chewed tobacco. "If he got fresh with you," she said, "you had to think twice before slapping his face."

I have a friend who's very cautious. He's so afraid of flying he refuses to ride the train. He's afraid an airplane will fall on it.

I know one guy who was so cautious he would only go out after dark because he was afraid of his own shadow.

This guy was afraid of his own shadow. Of course, he had reason to be—it looked exactly like him.

I know one guy who was so afraid of his own shadow that he made it walk ten paces behind him.

Another guy was so afraid of his own shadow, he used to stop and look in a window until it passed.

You show me a man who's afraid to take a chance, and I'll show you a man who will probably never win the lottery.

People who live in glass houses might as well answer the door.
—*Morey Amsterdam*

Parking is such street sorrow.—*Herb Caen*

A man in the house is worth two in the street.—*Mae West*

If at first you don't succeed, I'd stay away from skydiving.—*Milton Berle*

What is worth doing is worth the trouble of asking somebody to do it.
—*Ambrose Bierce*

You can lead a horse to water, but just stop to think how a wet horse smells.—*George Gobel*

. . .

If at first you don't succeed, appoint a committee and let them worry about it.

A stitch in time can sometimes save embarrassment.

Keep your eye on the ball, your nose to the grindstone, and your shoulder to the wheel. If you can work in that position, you're a better person than I am.

If you can't see the forest for the trees, try looking around for a forest that doesn't have any trees.

Monkey see, monkey do. I don't know what that means. I'm only putting it in here because I've seen it in other books.

Neither a borrower nor a lender be. That kind of kills any fun you were going to have with the stock market, doesn't it?

Do unto others before they get a chance to do unto you.

A penny saved is a penny earned. You don't have to take my word on that. . . . Call the IRS.

A rolling stone gathers no moss. How you react to that statement depends on whether or not you have a worthwhile use for moss.

You can lead a horse to water, but if you really want to make him drink, put out a bowl of beer nuts first.

If at first you don't succeed, start looking around for someone to blame.

A FEW CRAZY THOUGHTS

I still say if God had meant us to eat peanut butter, he would have given us Teflon gums.—*Robert Orben*

I came across a tribe of cannibals who'd been converted by Roman Catholic missionaries. Now, on Friday, they only eat fishermen.
—*Max Kaufman*

I'm going to memorize your name and throw my head away.
—*Oscar Levant*

I bought a tube of Krazy Glue and the label fell off.—*Jay Leno*

I just heard from Bill Bailey. He's not coming home.—*Henny Youngman*

The latest invention I've heard about is a toothpaste with built-in food particles for people who can't eat between every brushing.
—*Henny Youngman*

I like to skate on the other side of the ice.—*Steven Wright*

Luther Burbank crossed a potato with a sponge. He got something that tastes awful, but it holds a lot of gravy.—*Doodles Weaver*

I invented a square bathtub which cannot leave a ring. —*Jackie Vernon*

I had this great idea to make the Great Wall of China into a handball court.—*George Gobel*

Two kangaroos are talking to each other. One says, "Gee, I hope it doesn't rain today. I just hate it when the children play inside."—*Henny Youngman*

I'm an expert on Chinese food. When I eat it I only use one chopstick.
—*George Burns*

. . .

I always buy suits that are too small for me. Then when they don't fit, I don't feel obliged to go on a diet.

Today, you can go to a
gas station and find the
cash register open and
the toilets locked.
—*Joey Bishop*

I wore a turtleneck sweater once. When I lay on my back, I found out I couldn't roll over.

I went to a paint store once that had handicapped parking spaces for people who were color-blind.

I go to a very inexpensive doctor. He's an externist.

I know a guy who says he's going to be an atheist all his life, God willing.

This world is so unfair. Otherwise, why do the rich people have all the money?

My friend's fear of flying eventually killed him. At the airport, an insurance vending machine fell on him.

A friend of mine became a podiatrist. When he was going to medical school, he didn't want to buy the whole skeleton.

My mother always wanted a dishwasher, but we couldn't afford it. Dad bought her a bunch of paper plates and an eraser.

SILLY THINGS TO PONDER

What's right is what's left if you do everything else wrong.
—*Robin Williams*

What do you send a sick florist?—*Henny Youngman*

Has any turtle ever outlived the shaker of turtle food?—*Jerry Seinfeld*

Do you ever wonder if illiterate people get the full effect of alphabet soup? —*John Mendoza*

If you shoot at mimes, should you use a silencer?—*Steven Wright*

How come it's a penny for your thoughts, but you have to put in your 2-cents' worth? Somebody's making a penny.—*Steven Wright*

I'm desperately trying to figure out why kamikaze pilots wear helmets.
—*Dave Edison*

How come when you mix flour and water together you get glue? And when you add eggs and sugar, you get a cake? Where does the glue go?
—*Rita Rudner*

Did you ever notice when you blow in a dog's face, he gets mad at you, but when you take him in a car, he sticks his head out the window?
—*Steve Bluestein*

. . .

What's another word for *thesaurus*?

What time is check-out time in a roach motel?

Why don't fish have to wait an hour after they eat to go swimming again?

What I want to know is: when Noah had the two flies on the ark, why didn't he swat them?

If the law of gravity is ever repealed, which way would we all fall?

What happens if you want to become a tree surgeon, then discover that you can't stand the sight of sap?

If love makes the world go round, why can't I save a few bucks and get it to run my car?

If the number 8 decided to grow long hair and wear an earring, would it then become an odd number?

When you get right down to it, don't you always find something in the last place you look for it?

If you put a coffee table in your bedroom, would it keep you up at night?

If God gets amnesia, does that make Him an atheist?

NAMES INDEX